Worship *in* Light
of the Cross

Worship *in* Light *of the* Cross

Meditations *for* Lent

JOHN INDERMARK

UPPER
ROOM BOOKS®
NASHVILLE

Cover: LUCAS Art & Design, Jenison, MI
Cover art: Masterfile Images
Interior design: Perfect Type, Nashville, Tennessee

LIBRARY OF CONGRESS CATALOGING-IN-PUBLICATION DATA
Names: Indermark, John, 1950– author.
Title: Worship in light of the cross : meditations for Lent / John Indermark.
Description: Nashville : Upper Room Books, 2016.
Identifiers: LCCN 2016005508 | ISBN 9780835815727 (print) | ISBN 9780835815734 (mobi) | ISBN 9780835815741 (epub)
Subjects: LCSH: Lent—Meditations. | Bible—Meditations.
Classification: LCC BV85 .I454 2016 | DDC 242/.34—dc23
LC record available at https://lccn.loc.gov/2016005508

CONTENTS

WEEK THREE
Confession: Honest to God | 43

WEEK FOUR
Proclamation: Gospel as Truth-Telling | 57

WEEK FIVE
Creed: Owning the Faith | 71

WEEK SIX
Response: Stepping Out | 85

HOLY WEEK
Sacrament: Recognizing God | 99

Leader's Guide | 109

Notes | 125
About the Author | 126

ACKNOWLEDGMENTS

Acknowledgments convey a sense of gratitude and indebtedness to others. In terms of how this book has come to be, I am indebted to a great many folks in my recent and distant past—those who have played significant roles in bringing this book to the light of day and to whom great thanks are due. While not exhaustive of all I could name, I want to single out the following individuals:

- Jeannie Crawford-Lee, Acquisitions Editor at Upper Room Books at the time of this project's approval, whose advocacy made another book with Upper Room Books possible for me;

- Rita Collett, editor at Upper Room Books, who has edited my work for over twenty years and whose labor in every instance made their published form far better than their drafted starts.

Those to whom I am likewise grateful for roles that stretch much farther back in time, for shaping my experience and views of worship and its grounding in the light of the cross:

- Pastor Jesse Pollmann and Rev. Dr. Oscar Rumpf, whose Lenten midweek services at Salvator Evangelical and Reformed United Church of Christ during my youth and young adulthood shed considerable light on the centrality of the cross not only for worship but discipleship;

- From among my professors at Eden Seminary: Dr. Hale Schroer, who elevated the role of liturgy far beyond pre- and post-sermon filler; and Rev. Robert Tabscott, who insisted that preaching identify "where the rubber meets the road" in making clear the biblical witness's intersection with daily life and societal concerns no matter the cost;

- Metaline Falls United Church of Christ, my first parish, that gave me the freedom and privilege to lead worship, make the mistakes novices inevitably make, and steadfastly return to gather each Sunday with a pastor who was still finding his way and voice.

- And to Judy, my wife and companion and sometimes editor, whose own love of liturgy traces like mine to our common background in the Evangelical and Reformed tradition that even now shapes where we find ourselves on Sunday mornings and midweek in Lent.

FOREWORD

Many Christians and churches observe Lent with special services (Ash Wednesday, midweek, Holy Week) and/or a Sunday worship series. These liturgical experiences often focus in theme or scriptural text on Jesus' cross. The question is, do we simply make Lent fit into liturgical structures that remain unaffected by what looms before Jesus and his disciples in Jerusalem? Or does the journey recalled in Lent's movement toward the cross impact and transform worship and its varied components? In other words, how can the cross shed light on what we do in worship and why—not just in this season but in every season?

Worship in Light of the Cross has two underlying purposes as a devotional resource for individuals and communities. First, this book aims to link the Lenten journey before you with worship that is thoroughly grounded in the repercussions of the cross. Second, this book bids you to discover in such cross-formed worship what it means to be a disciple of the Christ we confess not only risen but crucified.

Worship in Light of the Cross will engage those purposes through daily readings that begin on Ash Wednesday and conclude on Easter Sunday. Each reading will reflect on a brief scripture highlighted for that day, followed by a related prayer or spiritual exercise.

Take a closer look at the preceding Contents pages. You will notice that the readings are organized in weeks on the basis of traditional components of corporate worship: Processional, Gathering, Invocation, Confession, Proclamation, Creed,

Response, and Sacrament. Each week opens and closes with readings evoked by narratives that either take place on Good Friday or that directly address the meaning of the cross. The other four readings, drawn from both Old and New Testaments, relate more generally to that week's worship component.

Six readings a week (with the exception of Holy Week) create a weekly sabbath day with no reading. For groups, that would ideally be the day for a group session. The Leader's Guide (page 109) provides suggestions for engaging this book in a group. If you are not part of a group experience, consider this weekly sabbath as an opportunity to review the week's readings and your reflections on them. You may find that the weekly questions and exercises in the Leader's Guide provide the basis for your sabbath review.

Whether you are reading this book as part of a group or as an individual discipline, set aside a time each day when you can prayerfully open yourself to the highlighted scripture, read and reflect on the ensuing reading, and use the closing prayer or spiritual exercise. This book is not intended to be read through in one sitting. Setting a discipline of one reading per day provides an opportunity for deeper engagement with the material and its connection with your own journey through Lent.

This book's orienting the components of worship to the cross has deep roots in Christian tradition. Perhaps the most striking example of this orientation can be seen in the architecture of many of the world's great cathedrals. Beyond all the apparent differences in furnishings and structural flourishes, most cathedrals share a simple foundational "footprint": They are built in the form of a cross. To enter into worship was literally to enter into a cross. Architectural styles may change, but worship remains imprinted by the cross. May this book deepen your exploration of that imprint on your practice of worship and on your walk as a disciple of Jesus Christ.

PROCESSIONAL
ASH WEDNESDAY

Pilgrims

Read Psalm 122 and Luke 9:51.

Pilgrim. Hear that word around Thanksgiving, and an initial association may be with folks who landed on Plymouth Rock and celebrated a harvest feast with the first Americans. But what image—what *vocation*—might the word *pilgrim* evoke for you on Ash Wednesday?

Luke tells us that Jesus "set his face to go to Jerusalem." The language reveals not only the direction Jesus takes but also the resolve with which he takes it. Beyond that, it is not simply *where* Jesus goes that matters here—it is *when.* He will enter Jerusalem in the week of Passover. Jesus' journey to Jerusalem is not a solitary act. Jesus joins thousands of pilgrims whose faces are set on observing Passover in Jerusalem. Such a pilgrimage identifies Jesus as a pious observer of centuries-old Jewish traditions. Many of the psalms, including Psalm 122, commemorate the journeys made by Jewish pilgrims to the holy city.

When Jesus makes this pilgrimage, he does so as part of a community bound by sacred memory and shared ritual. For this reason, the opening reading for *Worship in Light of the Cross* centers on the theme of pilgrims and pilgrimage. Like Jesus' Passover pilgrimage, during this season of Lent, you and I also make a journey bound by sacred memory and shared ritual. Like Jesus, indeed *with* Jesus, we are pilgrims on the road to Jerusalem.

The memories that accompany our journey grow out of Jesus' words and actions on his pilgrimage along with the ritualized traditions of Judaism that shaped Jesus' path. We engage in such remembrance to recall God's saving actions in our lives today. Memory that does not influence contemporary living is ineffectual nostalgia, no matter how fond or familiar the stories of Jesus may strike us.

The shared ritual that marks our journey as persons and communities of faith centers on worship. It matters little where we fall on the spectrums of worship as formal or informal, liturgical or "free-form," traditional or contemporary. It matters greatly, however, whether we allow our worship to be cruciform in shape. Worship that flees from the disruptive possibilities of the cross, whether out of naïve triumphalism or a fear of alienating people we'd like to fill our pews or subscribe our budgets, is empty ritual.

So on this day of ashes, set your face with Jesus toward Jerusalem and claim your vocation as pilgrim.

As I journey on this path, O God, open my understandings and practices of worship to the transformative possibilities of cross-formed faith. In Jesus Christ. Amen

WEEK ONE

Gathering
Forming Community

What if you gave a party and no one came? Would it still be a party? What if you formed a community, but no one gathered? Would it still be a community? What if you planned a liturgy, but no one showed up? Would it still be worship?

In spite of the value of individual study of scripture and private devotion, at some point the worship of God calls you to enter community. It bids you to gather with others—even if it be, in Jesus' oft-quoted words, simply where "two or three gather in my name" (Matt. 18:20, NIV).

This week's readings will explore some dynamics of worship's initial and initiating movement of gathering. The question before you will be this: What does it mean to gather with this particular community whose worship is shaped inescapably by the cross? The church does not engage naively in worship only to discover at the end that a cross enters the picture. This week's readings invite you to reflect on the how, the why, and the who (and by whom) of a gathering that announces up front that the light of the cross illumines the way ahead.

DAY 1 • *If and Then*

Read Matthew 16:24.

I suspect we prefer unconditional invitations to community. Whether we frame our hospitality in bywords of "open doors" or "wherever you are on life's journey," we seek to assure folks that they are welcome—and with good reason. Heaven knows there are plenty of places with the ecclesial equivalents of secret handshakes and moralistic slogans to gauge who is welcome to gather with "us" and who is not. I do not dispute the need for faith communities to be gracious and hospitable in their invitations to gather.

But as we listen to Matthew 16:24, we hear Jesus sounding a cautionary word about an *a priori* condition for all such gatherings and communities that bear the name of Jesus. The condition is simple: *If* we gather in order to follow Jesus, *then* our gathering cannot avoid Jesus' summons to take up the cross.

If and then. I admit this conditioning of faith with the words *if* and *then* seems a little harsh. Isn't grace supposed to winnow out the "oughts" and "have tos" of religion? Doesn't God love us—warts and all?

Yes.

But.

The God who gathers us in Jesus' name opens the door to *everyone* with a capital *E*. The God who gathers us in Jesus' example pronounces love for all creation. (See John 3:16 for the God who so loved the *world*.) When it comes to who is welcome in Christ's community, all the usual boundaries deployed to divide "us" from "them" are dismantled. However, the inclusivity of Jesus' invitation does not warrant an anything-goes approach. The community God gathers, radical in its gracious embrace of all, is equally radical in its formation in the shape of a cross.

"If any want to become my followers, let them deny themselves and take up their cross and follow me."

Every time we gather in worship and, to be frank, every time we gather as a community of faith for whatever purpose, those words demand our attention. Why? They provide the cross-shaped entry through which Jesus invites all to gather. We do not gather as a neighborhood club. We do not gather as a mutual admiration society of people who remind us of us. We gather in Jesus' name as those who would follow the Christ on the Jerusalem road.

> *Imagine the words of Matthew 16:24 ("If any want to become my followers, let them deny themselves and take up their cross and follow me") carved above the entryway of your sanctuary. Those words confront you each time you gather for worship. For you, would those words serve as a hurdle to overcome or as a light to show the way?*

DAY 2 • *The Plan*

Read Jeremiah 29:11.

I have yet to take advantage *of* (or be taken advantage of *by*) an invitation for a free weekend stay at a nice resort in exchange for a two-hour "presentation." Why? I believe I know the plan ahead of time. The issuer wants my signature on a purchase agreement for a time-share or property. I choose not to gather for the sales pitch, no matter how appealing the offer, because I know the plan.

In Jeremiah 29, the prophet addresses the first group of Jews shipped into exile in Babylon. You may think God's appeal to the exiles would be *Resist. Have nothing to do with the hated invaders and occupiers of the land. Put down no roots.* Instead, God bids the exiles to do quite the opposite: "Build houses . . . plant gardens" (v. 5). Raise families. And then, the most excruciating word of all: "Seek the welfare of the city where I have sent you into exile, and pray to the LORD on its behalf, for in its welfare you will find your welfare" (v. 7).

Pray for Babylon? Seek its welfare? The scandal of the latter command only magnifies when we consider the Hebrew word translated as "welfare": *shalom.* More often rendered as "peace," *shalom* encompasses a sense of wholeness of life. What makes for *shalom* includes all things that make life joyful and just; want does not exist and peace reigns.

What would make it possible for the exiles to accept such a difficult and offensive task as extending *shalom* to their captors? The plan behind all this, the plan God announces in verse 11, allows for that possibility. The plan is a future marked by hope. God seeks not the community's harm by engaging in this task but its own *shalom*. With such a plan, God seeks to form the scattered exiles into a new and renewing community.

Whenever the people of God gather today—for liturgy, for service—God's plan revealed through Jeremiah continues to form new and renewing community. God still gathers us to seek the *shalom* of our neighbors, even the ones who trespass against us. God still gathers us to live in hope, even in the midst of times that seem anything but hopeful.

That remains the plan that bids us gather . . . and worship . . . and live.

Call to mind one place in your life that seems bereft of hope or peace. Read Jeremiah 29:11. What do you hear God bringing to that place in these words?

DAY 3 • *Boundary Breaking*

Read Galatians 3:28.

"All of you are one in Christ Jesus." Really? Evidence to the contrary litters the church's history. We can easily see and reject the gross contradictions of Paul's assertion, at least when there is a safe distance involved. The cruelties of the Inquisition. The obscenities of Protestants and Catholics killing one another in the wake of the Reformation and more recently in Ireland. The stunning justification of slavery in the name of God in the United States.

But what happens when the contradictions to Paul's remarkable vision come in more subtle and respectable—and contemporary—guise? We may nod our heads in congenial assent when Paul asserts that there is no longer Jew or Greek, slave or free, male or female. Those matters have been settled, though pockets of resistance remain for leadership roles fully available to women in the church.

Still, if Paul were writing this epistle today, who would he identify as no longer irreconcilably separated but one in Christ, in spite of ongoing evidence to the contrary? Would "Jew or Greek" be supplanted by "straight or gay?" Would "slave or free" be rendered as "birth-certificated citizen or undocumented immigrant?" Would "male or female" be transposed into "the ones in your community for whom the sky is the limit" or "those whose place in community is limited by glass ceilings imposed by obstinate and antiquated traditions"?

Galatians 3:28 is not a historical curiosity as to what boundaries had to be broken in the first-century church to form authentic Christian community. Galatians 3:28 calls the twenty-first-century church to vigilance regarding boundaries that jeopardize the formation of authentic Christian community. What walls keep the whole of Christ's community from being gathered and empowered?

"There is no longer _____." Fill in the blank by naming the boundaries that divide Christ's body and exclude others from full participation in Christ's community. Paul speaks about the unequivocal light beaming from the cross in Galatians 2:19-20: "I have been crucified with Christ; and it is no longer I who live, but it is Christ who lives in me." Paul's identity as Jew and free and male do not vanish; in the cross, they become subsets of his overarching identity in Christ.

So God calls it to be with us. The differences between us do not disappear. They simply yield in divisive prerogative to the overarching result of grace for us and Christian community: We are all one in Christ.

Rewrite Galatians 3:28 to address boundaries you and your faith community may need to reconsider.

DAY 4 • *Counterintuitive*

Read 1 Corinthians 1:26-29.

Listening to Paul describe the community that God gathers in Corinth, we may think that God has a wicked sense of humor or, perhaps, that God never had to serve on an evangelism committee. Can you imagine the reaction on "invite a friend to church Sunday" if the pastor looked out over the old and new faces in the pews and solemnly intoned, "Not many of you are going to rival Einstein, not many of you are among the movers and shakers of this world—in fact, you're here because God is inclined toward the foolish and weak and despised." If I were that pastor, I'd be polishing up my resume for immediate distribution.

Yet, that is the gist of what Paul says—and not just to those long-ago Christians of Corinth. That is the gist of what Paul says to you and to me and to the congregations with whom we gather for worship and service. Now as then, God is by nature counterintuitive. As a result, so is the community God seeks to gather.

This shouldn't surprise any of us since it has been the story all along. We might have figured that God would choose a people with more clout and numerical impressiveness than a ragtag crew of Hebrew slaves on the lam from Pharaoh. Yet, how does God explain that peculiar choice? "It was not because you were more numerous than any other people that the LORD set his heart on you and chose you—for you were the fewest of all peoples. It was because the LORD loved you" (Deut. 7:7-8). We may have thought God would choose a Jewish champion to free the captives in Babylon so they could gather again in Jerusalem. Instead, God chose the Gentile Cyrus as his "anointed" (literally, "messiah") to set the captives free. (See Isaiah 44:28–45:1.)

God has this persistent habit of counterintuition when choosing the ones to gather into community and through whom God does the gathering. Put another way, God consistently exercises grace in the communities God forms.

When extended in our direction, grace feels great. When extended toward those with whom we differ or are in conflict— the ones we would never have chosen to gather with—grace may rub us the wrong way. But as First Corinthians points out, God's call gathers and forms community. And the cross, which embodies God's counterintuitive grace, gathers us all.

Where do you see examples of and need for God's counterintuitive grace in your worshiping community?

DAY 5 • *Search and Rescue*

Read Ezekiel 34:11-16.

My wife and I live in Washington state. Our home is located about thirteen miles as the seagull flies from the Cape Disappointment Coast Guard Station. Situated at the mouth of the Columbia River, the station routinely engages in search-and-rescue missions for mariners in distress. The need for search and rescue may owe to sudden and violent storms or incredibly poor judgment. But when a chopper crew lowers a gurney to retrieve people from a sinking boat or out of the sea, the Coast Guard does not ask them to fill out a questionnaire to ascertain their merit before being plucked to safety. When the searchers find those imperiled on the sea, they rescue them. Gathering them back to dry land precedes all else.

In my mind, the Cape Disappointment station serves as a contemporary metaphor for the God described in Ezekiel 34. Playing on the literal meaning in Hebrew of shepherd as "one who feeds," Ezekiel draws a stinging political contrast between God as shepherd who will feed Israel and Israel's previous "shepherds" whose misuse of power is depicted as their *feeding on* the flock. Beyond the vocation of feeding, however, Ezekiel portrays God's shepherding action in terms of gathering Israel from its scattering in exile. God engages in search and rescue.

Whether we speak of the Coasties at Cape Disappointment or Ezekiel's good shepherd, one truth holds for both. Search must precede rescue. Neither Coast Guard personnel nor Ezekiel's God can accomplish rescue without first heading out of port, leaving the comfort zone for the danger zone. In order to gather distressed mariners or scattered exiles, rescuers must first make their way to them, no matter the risk.

That truth can be a stumbling block to those of us in the church. We like to think everybody knows we are here and ready to help. But we leave it to them to find their way to us. That approach is fine when we talk about church shoppers. But what of folks struggling to keep their heads above water who don't know where to turn? How do we as individuals and communities of faith move into search mode as opposed to appearing to be the equivalent of religious department stores waiting for people to discover our bargains?

Consider Jesus' decision to enter Jerusalem despite storm warnings on the horizon. The community God will gather cannot remain in splendid Galilean isolation, far from Pilate and pious accusers. As with Ezekiel, the God Jesus reveals is on the move, searching out and gathering the scattered.

So God gathers us in worship to go and do likewise.

Who sought you out and gathered you into Christian community? Who may need you to search for them?

DAY 6 • *Transformed Relationship*

Read John 19:26-27.

Not all gatherings are ones we choose. I remember sitting in a courtroom to support a parishioner as her husband was being sentenced for sexually abusing their grandchild. I recall standing at the lectern of a packed high school gymnasium, presiding at the funeral of one of my son's best friends. Those gatherings arose from tragedies set into motion by human cruelty and youthful indiscretion gone irretrievably awry. Yet in those gatherings, some—myself included—found healing and new relationship with those whom we took our place beside.

So it was at the hill called Golgotha. Who would gather to keep vigil beneath Jesus' cross? Matthew and Mark attest that after Jesus' arrest, all the disciples "deserted him and fled." Even Luke, who indicates that "all his acquaintances" watched his crucifixion, adds the caveat that they did so "at a distance." Fear of gathering stilted community.

Only John's Gospel depicts a small cadre gathered beneath the cross, consisting of three women named Mary (mother of Jesus, her sister, and the Magdalene) and the follower whom John cryptically identifies as "the disciple whom [Jesus] loved." John does not state why they gather. Perhaps they hope for a last-minute reprieve. Perhaps they come to pay last respects to the one they followed in life. Perhaps . . . we just do not know. John simply reports that they gather.

But whatever brought them together, the fact of their gathering sets into motion a dramatic transformation in relationship. "Woman, here is your son. . . . Here is your mother." Much has been written and preached as to the theological import of these words of Jesus. Mary has been offered as signifying the church, the one who continues to "bear" Jesus to the world. The one Jesus loved is interpreted as a metaphor for disciples in every age beckoned to love and care for the church.

But beyond the theologizing, consider this. Two human beings, previously unconnected as family become family. Why? Because in their choosing to gather, even in a toxic environment, God transforms the relationship between them and forms new community.

Gathering for worship, gathering for any and every act of forming Christian community, draws its purest light from the cross. Why? Because the fundamental purpose for our gathering, and for God's gathering of us, is to celebrate the possibility of life rising out of death—and community rising out of isolation. Thanks be to God!

God, gather me to you and to others for the sake of the community you would form. Amen.

WEEK TWO

Invocation: Attending to the Holy

It may seem presumptuous, even manipulative, to invoke God's presence when we gather for worship. Isn't the Holy One already there? Must God wait in the wings until properly summoned, like Johnny Carson waiting on Ed McMahon's "Heeere's Johnny"?

The previous week of readings touched on God's initiating presence in the forming of faith's community. It follows then that invocation does not signify some magical conjuring to ensure that God makes an appearance. Invoking God, naming the Holy One, reminds us of whose presence and purpose gathers us in worship and sends us in service. Invocation serves as a hedge against worship reduced to self-improvement seminars or political workshops because invocation declares we do not gather first and foremost for the sake of our agendas. Invocation bids us attend to God in our midst.

The readings and reflections of this coming week challenge you to consider invocation's transformative possibility for worship and for discipleship. What does it mean to attend to the Holy One whom Jesus reveals as the *crucified God*?

DAY 1 • *Do You Not Fear God?*

Read Luke 23:39-41.

The concept of the fear of God has fallen onto hard times. The admirable desire to lift up grace and love as preeminent in God's character casts a suspicious eye on faith grounded in fear. Doesn't 1 John 4:18 counsel us that "There is no fear in love, but perfect love casts out fear"? As a consequence, many have come to view and often discard the fear of God as an antiquated relic of primitive religion that has not yet seen the light of "what a friend we have in Jesus." But in doing so, have they overly domesticated the sense of God's holiness?

In his book *The Brothers Karamazov*, the Russian writer Dostoevsky makes this observation through one of the book's characters: "Without God. . . . Everything is permitted."[1] On the hill called Golgotha outside of Jerusalem, it appears that everything *is* permitted. Setting aside whatever theologies we carry about the nature of Jesus' divinity, at that place, authorities execute an innocent man. The only fear present seems to be the one that religious and political leaders hope to impose as a deterrent on any who would trouble the status quo that assures their positions. But as sometimes happens in the Gospels and in Luke in particular, an outsider, an outcast, cuts to the heart of the matter. The penitent thief cries out, "Do you not fear God?" to the third man being crucified who spends his dying moments mocking Jesus. In the midst of this unworshipful gathering marked by smugness and callousness to human suffering, the penitent utters the protest that is in truth an invocation demanding attention to the holy in our midst: Do you not fear God?

The invocation not only cries out against the spiritual and political blindness that sanctions the killing of an innocent. The penitent ask to be remembered in Jesus' kingdom, a request that reveals an assessment of his crucified companion as much more than a guiltless victim. The invocation of the penitent challenges those who gather at the cross then and those of us who will gather now in its shadow in the season of Lent to attend to God's holiness. That holiness hopes to generate a sense of awe that moves beyond our experience of worship into the transformation of our lives and ethics.

When and to what purpose, O God, do I need to hear anew: "Do you not fear God?" Amen.

DAY 2 • *Who Is This?*

Read Matthew 8:18-27.

In the movie *Butch Cassidy and the Sundance Kid*, the titled characters initially enjoy an easy time with posses that fail to organize or that give up their efforts to trail them. All that changes, however, when the Union Pacific Railroad hires a new group to pursue the outlaws. Their dogged persistence in tracking Butch and the Kid through the remainder of the film results in the duo's repeated exclamations when the pursuers come into view: "Who are those guys?"

In the Gospel narrative at hand, a similar sense of exasperation and mystery culminates in the disciples' wondering aloud about this rabbi who stills a raging storm on Galilee's sea. Their bewilderment may have started earlier in the episode when Jesus declares some rather off-putting words to one who would follow and another whom Matthew identifies as a disciple already. Telling the dead to bury their own dead does not sound like something someone overly anxious about making sure the pew count or pledging units continue to increase would say.

The disciples often do not fare well in the Gospel portrayals. Time and again, they misunderstand what Jesus says; they ask for the wrong things; or they head for the hills when trouble comes. But here, their ankles still submerged in water that nearly swamps the boat, it sounds like they get it just about right: "What sort of man is this?" We might even say that their question is an invocation. In their state of awe at what has just happened, they recognize that they stand in the presence of One who is Other, who is holy. When we stand in the presence of mystery, maybe a question or an admission of not knowing serves as the most appropriate and faithful of responses. Why? It invokes wonder about holy possibilities and where they might lead. "Who is this?" remains an ongoing question for the disciples about the One they follow.

- Who is this Jesus—who did not follow the adage of discretion being the better part of valor when it came to overturning tables in the Temple?

- Who is this Jesus—who told would-be defenders to put away their swords rather than use them when accusers came for him?

This same question calls us to attend to the holy possibilities in our lives and choices as we who follow Jesus journey through the season of Lent.

- Who is this Jesus—who counsels love of enemies rather than revenge?

- Who is this Jesus—who forgives while calling us to be forgiving?

- Who is this Jesus—who still reveals himself in human form in the poor and vulnerable?

Open me, O God, to who you are that I may better understand who you call me to be. Amen.

DAY 3 • *Holy Grounding*

Read Exodus 3:1-6.

Have you ever seen a bush burning without being consumed and then heard the voice of God speaking from its midst, calling you by name? The singularity of some biblical narratives can make them hard to identify with—or leave us longing for God to come to us in such distinctive and indisputable ways. After all, we would like to have some certainty about this faith thing. We wouldn't mind a burning bush experience once in a while.

However, the fiery bush is not the core of this story. It functions merely to catch Moses' attention to ready him for its (literally) underlying affirmation: "The place on which you are standing is holy ground." I have never encountered a bush burning without being consumed, but I have known what it means to stand on holy ground—a place where I have received gracious assurance or had my eyes opened to the presence of the Holy One.

Holy ground represents a recognition, an invocation, that hopefully strikes us each time we gather for worship. We need not limit holy ground only to consecrated sanctuaries. All manner of settings other than traditional Sunday morning rendezvous places can invoke the remembrance and hope of encountering the God of our fathers and mothers, of Abraham and Sarah, and whomever else we may name in our faith's family lineage. But whether the sanctuary lies nestled in a cathedraled forest or in a white-frame edifice filled with hardwood pews, the function of holy ground remains. This place invokes our sense of standing in God's presence.

I would be remiss to ignore Moses' reaction to this invitation to stand on holy ground and attend to the holy Presence who speaks. "Moses hid his face, for he was afraid to look at God." What prompted Moses' fear? One answer appeals to traditions of not daring to look upon God that occur in other Old Testament encounter stories. But another possible answer helps us understand why holy ground resonates with grace as much as awe. In the preceding chapter of Exodus, Moses has killed a man. The commandments Moses will later receive don't allow much leeway or wiggle room about murderers.

Yet, what happens in the encounter presented in this reading? God bids Moses to come and stand on holy ground. Moses may have expected judgment and punishment for his unholy past, but holy ground provides grace.

Holy ground still serves that providential function in our lives. God invokes the gift of holy ground and presence to all in need of sanctuary, even the most unexpected or seemingly undeserving. Even Moses. Even me. Even you.

What, for you, serves as holy ground? What grace does it bear to you?

DAY 4 • *The Anointed*

Read Mark 8:27-33.

The day of confirmation examination arrived. Forty or so white-robed confirmands sat before a packed sanctuary. Pastor Prell read aloud questions from the *Evangelical Catechism*, then called on one of the hands that thrust up in confident hope that the memorized answer could be recalled before peers, parents, and gathered congregation. The longer the catechism answer, the fewer hands shot up. It was a red badge of knowledge to be one of the chosen few who answered the tough questions correctly. Some among us were not so confident and waited on the easy questions in hopes of catching a break. While Pastor Prell could be strict, he revealed his compassionate heart when he called on one such boy to answer the extra-catechetical question about where Jesus was born.

Jerusalem.

Those of us with an overabundance of adolescent smugness gave ourselves an invisible pat on the back and stifled giggles. We knew the right answers to the hard questions, and this guy couldn't even get this one? But in the years since my confirmation, I have learned something more about faith. Having the right answer is not enough. Just ask Peter: Knowing the right answer means nothing without understanding its implications.

Peter would have passed that day's catechism question with flying colors: *Question:* Who is Jesus? *Answer:* Jesus is the Messiah, a Hebrew term that like its corresponding word in Greek *christos* (or Christ) means "anointed." I can even imagine the other disciples, who had answered Jesus' prior question of "who do people say that I am" with the equivalent of hearsay, now high-fiving Peter for having nailed it with his orthodox ID of Jesus as the Anointed One of God.

But in some ways, Peter was farther off in his answer than my confirmation companion who uttered *Jerusalem.* At least Jerusalem and Bethlehem are barely five miles apart. The "anointed one" whom Peter expected was light years distant from the "anointed one" that Jesus had come to be. The ensuing exchange makes that discrepancy clear. Peter rebukes Jesus' version of messiah, and Jesus deconstructs Peter's watered-down, crossless version of messiah with "Get behind me, Satan!" Having the right answer doesn't guarantee the right faith.

Invoking the name of Christ, the Anointed One, can become a dangerously formulaic recitation in worship or prayer. The encounter between Peter and Jesus on the way to Caesarea Philippi reminds us that even the most orthodox of confessions can be empty of power and truth. Invoking the name of Christ summons us to attend to worship and discipleship inseparably linked to the cross.

Who do you say that Jesus is?

How can you bring greater mindfulness of the cross when you invoke the title of "Christ" in prayer, in worship, in service?

DAY 5 • *Surprise!*

Read 1 Kings 19:1-13.

Poor Elijah! Queen Jezebel swears vengeance against him so the prophet hightails it to the wilderness in hopes he might die in peace, the last of God's prophets.

Two things interrupt his pity party. First, an angel disturbs his suicidal slumber with two meals and word of a journey. The second interruption occurs after Elijah settles in to a cave on Mount Horeb after a journey of forty days. Horeb is another name for Sinai, the mountain where Moses received the commandments. And the *forty* days? Israel's wilderness sojourn following the Sinai experience lasted *forty* years. So with all that Exodus tradition washing over him, Elijah hears a voice that promises an appearance by God. Naturally, the expectation will be of God's coming in wind and earthquake and fire. Weren't those the accompaniments of God's first Sinai revealing? (Read Exodus 19:16-18.) And isn't God the same yesterday, today, and forever?

Apparently not.

Wind blows, earthquake shakes, fire rages—but no God. Instead, God chooses a new entrance: "a sound of sheer silence" or in the more familiar King James rendering, "a still small voice." In that surprising self-disclosure, God goes on to disabuse Elijah of his mistaken notion that he alone remains a faithful prophet. God sets Elijah back on his prophetic path.

So what sort of invocation does this narrative provide, particularly in the season of Lent? It announces that the God in whose name we gather is a God who may surprise us and shatter our presumptions about life in general and about God in particular. We cannot shut God up in neat boxes of theology or liturgy that we trot out for pious show and put away when gospel truths like cross-bearing become inconvenient.

Some people use this scripture to support the primacy of quiet, unobtrusive experiences of God ("sheer silence, still small voice") over the extravagant equivalents of wind and earthquake and fire when it comes to spiritual encounter. As someone who falls on the introverted side of personality tests, that would be my preference. But this story is not about invoking a God who favors the more quieted among us. This story testifies to the God who refuses to be locked in to any one tradition or liturgical style. The God who surprises Elijah on Horeb is the God who retains the freedom to be God in God's own image. May we open our lives and faith to the God still capable of holy and redemptive surprise.

Where has God surprised you in the past—and where does God need to surprise you now?

DAY 6 • *Truly*

Read Mark 15:39.

Of all the places: Golgotha, a place used by Roman occupiers to dispose of the worst of the worst. Of all the people: a centurion, charged with overseeing that day's disposal of two thieves and a would-be king. We would not expect to encounter the Holy at such a place and time. Nor would we expect the officer assigned with executing Rome's enemies to confess one such foe as somehow bearing a familial connection to the Holy. Yet Mark's Gospel culminates in an extraordinary invocation that invites all within earshot to attend to the Holy One now crucified. Truly.

I realize the centurion's confession is fraught with textual uncertainty since the New Revised Standard Version offers an option to the confession "Truly this man was God's Son." The option reads, "Truly this man was *a* son of God." The grammar in ancient manuscripts of Mark can be rendered either way. Some interpreters suggest the latter reading places the centurion's confession in the realm of mocking irony.

The witness of Matthew and Luke about this centurion suggests that his confession in Mark is not sounded in a mocking tone akin to the scoffers gathered that day. And even if we find out someday that the centurion *actually* said "*a* son of God" rather than *the* son of God—even that invocation carries weight. Why? In the ugliness of that place, where human life was callously taken, the centurion's "truly this man" serves as a not-so-subtle rebuttal of Golgotha's attempted dehumanization of its victims. *This man* serves as a crack in the façade of authoritarianism that eliminates individuality and lumps all enemies into one faceless mass. The phrase *a son of God* could convey a defiant invocation that life belongs to its Author and not its executioner.

The alternate translation of the confession, "truly this man was God's Son," carries even more power. It is not simply in this unholy of places that we encounter the Holy One but in the very One who has been stripped and nailed and hung to die. For this reason, the season of Lent and worship that adheres to Lent's journey to Jerusalem is crucial. If our invocations call us to attend to the God who comes among us, then they beckon us to take our place alongside the centurion—to attend, with him, to the Holy One incarnate in the most unlikely of places and unlikely of persons. Truly.

Gracious God, may I recognize you in others—and love them accordingly. Amen.

WEEK THREE

Confession: Honest to God

Come on now. You stand in the presence of the One who spun worlds into being, the God who Psalm 139 confesses "discern(s) my thoughts from far away." Is there a reason not to be honest to God, to steer clear of the not-so-gentle art of confession in the presence of the One who knows you better than you know yourself?

You need not understand confession solely as acknowledgment of sin. Confession includes that but goes deeper. Confession is about being honest to God. To be honest about your sin is a good and needful thing. But sin is not the be-all and end-all of honesty to God. In confession you speak with God in forthright honesty about the totality of your life: its pain, its unfairness, its abounding joy. Confession always involves willingness to bring the whole of life's experiences into the presence, hearing, and compassion of God. The psalms of Israel provide a rich example for how such honesty may be diversely expressed in the context of faith. But they are not the only places where persons cry out to God in absolute frankness and honesty. This week's readings lift up such voices for the sake of evoking your honesty to God.

Confession is good for the soul.

DAY 1 • *Baring the Heart*

Read Matthew 26:36-44.

Do we pray only what we guess God wants to hear from us? Or do we pray what cries out to be heard by God?

Granted, most of our prayers do not arise in contexts akin to Gethsemane's dark night of the soul. There is nothing wrong with routine and ordinariness in prayers invoked at meals or bedtimes or whatever times we customarily set aside for conversation of the heart with God. But moments do come when crises and tragedies that shake the foundations of our lives sweep away the routine and the ordinary, confronting us with the unsettling truth of our mortality. What do you pray when a friend calls to tell you that your son is in an ambulance in the aftermath of a car accident? What do you pray when the doctor intones "cancer" and "terminal" in the same sentence? What do you pray when . . . well, when you stand or kneel in your personal Gethsemane?

One reaction in the face of such chaotic disruption is silence. Our loss for words is more than understandable in such moments. On those occasions, the affirmation of Romans 8:26 that the Spirit intercedes for us "with sighs too deep for words" may bring comfort and empowerment. But sometimes we persist in silence, particularly in God's direction. Caught between wonderings as to why God has brought this upon us and a desire not to speak our mind to God frankly, we still our voice. We curb our words. We cease our prayers.

Gethsemane holds that option. Jesus can kneel down among the olive trees and hold his tongue and spirit. Had he not done what God desired him to do? *So why this? Why me?* Why bother saying anything at this point? Such silence, however, would be dishonest by withholding from God what is most pressing, most urgent. In Gethsemane, grieved and agitated as Matthew reveals Jesus to be, Jesus breaks the silence. He does not spare God from the agony he feels, an agony that in some manuscripts of Luke has Jesus sweating drops of blood. He does not bargain. "If it is possible" is followed by "your will be done." Jesus bares his heart in honesty to God. Jesus confesses the truth of his life.

Confession, whether in personal spiritual pilgrimage or corporate worship, serves that same purpose. Confession aims to move our words and spirits in the direction of honesty to God. We do not pray hoping to guess correctly what God wants to hear. We pray to bare our hearts and lives before God as Jesus did in Gethsemane. We pray out of the truth of our lives and those of our neighbors in hopes of God's gracious hearing and response.

At this moment, what bids you to bare yourself in utterly honest prayer before God?

DAY 2 • *Release*

Read Psalm 32:1-5.

In his version of the Bible titled *The Message*, Eugene Peterson offers an intriguing turn of phrase in the counsel of the risen Christ to his disciples in John 20:23. "If you don't forgive sins, what are you going to do with them?" The context there is forgiveness extended toward others regarding their sin. Let me suggest a paraphrase that relates a parallel truth: "If you don't confess sins, what will those sins do with you?"

Psalm 32:3-4 bluntly answers that question. The imagery employed by the psalmist ranges from a body wasting away to strength sapped by summer's heat. In other words, sin withers us from the inside out. Like the withholding of forgiveness from another that undermines relationship and community, the unwillingness to confess our sin corrodes our spirit and distances us from the One who seeks our healing and restoration.

The discipline of confessing sin, like that of extending forgiveness to others, can be hard for many reasons. Shame may intimidate us and make us reticent to confess, convincing us that no one has ever sinned as we have. On the opposite side of the spectrum—but equally debilitating—pride may lull us into thinking we have a corner on the righteousness market with no need for apology to anyone, including God. Perhaps most dangerous of all, fear works against confession. If the image of God stamped on our being is one of a deity full of wrath and poised to pounce in judgment upon the slightest imperfection, we may shy away from acknowledgment of anything that we presume would call hellfire and brimstone down upon us. Ironically, confession provides release from these captivities of our spirits.

Confession releases us from shame as we let go of that which tells us we have no worth and find restoration in the grace that affirms our truest identity as beloved children of God. Confession releases us from pride, setting us free from the never-ending attempts to convince others and ourselves of our blamelessness in all things. Above all else, confession releases us from fear. The One to whom we confess is not the "gotcha" God who gleefully waits for us to slip. We confess to the One revealed most clearly on the cross. Our confession opens us to the God whose unconditional love knows no bounds and goes to all lengths to embrace us.

"Happy are those," begins Psalm 32. Happy are those who find release from shame and pride and fear. Happy are those whose risk of honesty to God in confession is met with forgiveness and grace and empowerment for new life.

May you experience such happiness following confession.

Where, O God, does shame, pride, or fear hold me back from honest confession to you? Help me find release in you. Amen.

DAY 3 • *Intercession*

Read Genesis 18:17-33.

Ionce saw a lawyer named Bryan Stevenson interviewed on television about the release of his book *Just Mercy*.[2] In one part of the book, Stevenson describes his work in overturning the conviction of an African American man who had been placed on death row *prior* to his trial. In the interview, Stevenson discloses that at the beginning of the appeals process, the judge who had presided at the original trial and had converted the jury's original life sentence into a death sentence called Stevenson and advised him not to take this case. The lawyer chose not to follow the judge's counsel. Stevenson's legal intercession for Walter McMillian resulted in the undoing of an extraordinary injustice.

What would have happened if Stevenson had deferred to the judge's urging? What if the judge's status as an authority figure had persuaded the lawyer not to intercede? Fortunately, in this case, the "what if" questions are rendered moot. Bryan Stevenson interceded.

Abraham has just received the assurance of extraordinary blessing for himself and his wife in the covenantal promise of heirs and land. We might think that Abraham would tread cautiously in any further words with God so as not to jeopardize this favorable arrangement. We might think that Abraham has been promised so much he would be wise not to ask for anything more. But he does. Only he does not ask for himself. When God brings Abraham into the loop about Sodom and Gomorrah's "grave sin" and the implicit threat of their destruction, Abraham intercedes. Abraham's opening, "Will you indeed sweep away the righteous with the wicked?"

becomes the prelude to intercession that sounds like an auction in reverse: "Suppose there are fifty . . . forty-five . . . forty . . . thirty . . . twenty . . . ten. . . . "

Nothing suggests that Abraham has ever visited these cities or knows the people for whom he pleads. It is one thing to intercede for a friend or a loved one. But strangers? That may be the point of the story, for tucked away in its opening is the disclosure of Abraham's covenantal role: "*All* the nations of the earth shall be blessed in him" (emphasis added). All: not just the upright and decent ones, not just the ones who worship and vote as we do. All the nations will find blessing in Abraham. As a result, Abraham intercedes with God for the likes of Sodom and Gomorrah.

It is not the last time such honest-to-God confession in the form of intercession takes place. Consider Golgotha. Executioners nail. Opponents jeer. And what does the crucified Jesus do? Intercede. "Father, forgive them" (Luke 23:34).

So tell me: For whom do you intercede?

Who stands in need of your intercession in prayer? in action? Intercede!

DAY 4 • *The Woman Who Schooled Jesus*

Read Matthew 15:21-28.

You sometimes hear the phrase used in the context of basketball. A player with the ball executes a crossover dribble or another maneuver that leaves the defender behind, grasping at air. The defender has learned a lesson—*he got schooled!*

So who gets schooled in today's reading from Matthew? The presumptive candidates would be the disciples. They have a track record in the Gospels for misunderstanding that is both maddening and hopeful. Maddening in that they have the clear advantage of face-to-face time with Jesus to get things right. Hopeful, in that the church's origins in the likes of them suggests God can work through our stumblings and miscalculations in faith.

But the disciples do not get schooled.

The next likely candidate would be this woman who shouts for mercy for her child. Jesus' initial silence in the wake of her cries might have been enough to send other folks to seek help elsewhere. But Jesus' ignoring her does not succeed in "schooling" her on her place or lack thereof. Nor does the disciples' ensuing request for Jesus to send her and her incessant bellowing away. At this point, we might have thought or hoped that Jesus would tell the disciples, as he later did when children were brought to him (Matthew 19:14), that to *such as her the kingdom of heaven belongs.* But Jesus doesn't say that. In fact, it sounds like Jesus excludes her from the circle of those his ministry would embrace: "I was sent only to the lost sheep of the house of Israel."

And then it gets worse. When the woman throws herself at Jesus' feet and asks for help, his response compares her and her child to dogs. This common retort for Jews of Jesus' era to make against Canaanites implies that Jesus wishes to "school" her on her place.

But the one who would be schooled by Jesus now schools him. "Yes, Lord, yet even the dogs eat the crumbs that fall from their masters' table." The one who came as embodiment of God's compassion is now schooled in the persistent art of compassion by this woman. And Jesus, to his great credit, knows truth and trust when he hears it confessed. The woman's child receives healing, and he affirms her faith.

Whose presence among us, currently ignored as distracting or annoying or out of place, can school us in the truth-telling of Christian compassion if only we would break our silence, if only we would be as quick to listen as to speak? How does this woman school us in what it means to pray and act with compassion that will not take *no* or give *no* for an answer?

For whose goodwill did you persist in prayer and discipleship this day, this week?

DAY 5 • *Outcry*

Read Exodus 2:23-25.

When have you needed to get something off your chest so badly that you blurted it out? Anger can provoke our outcries. So can grief. We may cry out in the presence of others, or our outcries may erupt in solitude. In either case, such cries demand airing. The cry must be let out lest it roil within and consume us. The cry must be let out if it's to be heard—if only by the wind.

The Israelites raise such an outcry. Two elements of their situation merit special attention. First, the outcry follows the death of Pharaoh, the one who had forgotten Joseph and enslaved the Israelites. The cry rises from a moment of opportunity or desperation, fearing that the one who once ordered the slaughter of their male children will now be replaced by another even worse. In either case, the Israelites cry out for help. Second, the narrator does not note that they direct their outcry to God, much less that it is a prayer. The text merely affirms that God hears their cry for help. God hears, remembers, looks, . . . and takes notice.

So if the Israelites had not cried out, would God have responded to their situation? The text only testifies to the outcry of the Israelites rising up to God as prelude to deliverance.

How does the Israelites' outcry relate to this week's concern of confession as honesty before God? On one level, it reasserts the importance of frankness in speaking the truth of our lives and the lives of those around us into the redemptive hearing of God. While Exodus does not provide the specifics of the Israelites' outcry, these verses connote pain and mourning. An outcry for help in a time of pain and mourning does not suggest subtlety or timidity but candor and directness. On a second level, the outcry of the Israelites, while not specified in Exodus as direct address to God, speaks grace to us. Occasions that provoke our outcries may, in the moment, trigger expressions not consciously associated with prayer. Exodus 2 suggests God hears such cries and groaning whether spawned by grief or outrage at injustice or mourning even when we do not knowingly direct them to God. When we cry out the truth of our lives and those of our neighbors in all honesty, the gospel of Exodus proclaims this: God hears, remembers, looks, . . . and takes notice.

Today, I cry out for help for. . . .

DAY 6 • *Is Anybody There?*

Read Mark 15:34.

You may have heard the saying, "There are no atheists in foxholes." But I suspect we would find plenty of agnostics. When the world is collapsing, when usual supports are stripped away, when suffering seems interminable, when death appears imminent: doubts and wonderings about God's presence naturally arise.

Is anybody there?

In his book *Night,* Elie Wiesel relates a story about his time in Auschwitz. Two men and a youth were hanged before the assembled inmates. While the two men died quickly, it took almost half an hour before the youth finally ceased struggling and died. During the ordeal, Wiesel heard someone standing behind him ask, "Where is God?"[3]

Is anybody there?

Lest we dismiss the question overheard by Wiesel as devoid of faith, recall the cry raised by Jesus on the cross: "My God, my God, why have you forsaken me?" The question quotes Psalm 22's opening verse, a psalm whose second half offers trustful praise of God's deliverance. Some take that to mean that Jesus asserts the message of the whole psalm by quoting its opening salvo. But there is a subtle trap in rushing to the end of that psalm without lingering in its beginning, a trap akin to skipping from Christmas to Easter in order to avoid the hard questions and harder calls of Lent. It is the trap that wants all of life to be triumphs and happy faces with no acknowledgment of life's shadowed and forsaken corners. Jesus utters the first verse of Psalm 22 because forsakenness confesses the honest-to-God truth of his life in that moment.

But in doing so, Jesus' confession of that moment's forsakenness becomes an extraordinary confession of faith. Why? Jesus does not forsake God. His cry of "my God" holds on to God even in his confession of experiencing abandonment.

Worship formed in light of the cross empowers us to hold on to God even when we wonder *Is anybody there?* Sometimes we believe that we enter worship (and faith) with all questions answered, all doubts removed, and all grievings and resentments carefully hidden in order to please God with our sunny dispositions. Jesus' honest-to-God confession at Golgotha sets a different tone. In worship, we come to God as we are—doubts, wonderings, and questions included. Nevertheless, we will not let go of God.

Which returns us to Wiesel's story. After the man behind him had asked again, "Where is God now" in this horrific incident, Wiesel confesses: "I heard a voice in myself answer, 'Where is he? He is here. He is hanging there on the gallows.'" Honest *to* God.

Teach me, O God, the courage to confess faith and doubt to you in all honesty. Amen.

WEEK FOUR

Proclamation: Gospel as Truth-Telling

No, this chapter is not reserved for preachers and traveling evangelists. While proclamation of the gospel is a function traditionally bestowed on ordained folk, it would be a tragic misunderstanding to conclude that they alone bear this vocation.

God entrusts proclamation of the gospel to the people of God. Such proclamation entails another facet of last week's focus. While confession hinges on our honesty to God, proclamation of the gospel involves speaking honestly to one another and to ourselves about the gift and call of discipleship. Proclamation of the gospel is not a religious sales job, nor does it involve scoring theological points against those with whom we disagree. Proclamation of the gospel is telling and living the truth of what it means to follow the God revealed in Jesus.

This week's readings bring a variety of perspectives regarding the truths to be told in the gospel's proclamation. No one-size-fits-all answer works when considering what constitutes such proclamation. Rather, the gospel's proclamation relies on a diversity of truth-tellings in order to address the contexts in which individuals and communities find themselves.

DAY 1 • *A Fool's Errand*

Read 1 Corinthians 1:18-25.

In Psalms and Proverbs, *fool* and *folly* are not terms of endearment. Quite the opposite. "Fools say in their hearts, 'There is no God'" (Ps. 14:1). "Like a dog that returns to its vomit is a fool who reverts to his folly" (Prov. 26:11).

So why does Paul, steeped in Judaism and doubtless familiar with these disparaging associations, assert that the message of the cross is foolishness? And why does Paul further disclose that God's choosing us as gospel proclaimers is more foolishness?

In the eyes of what passes for wisdom and power in this world, what the church proclaims really is foolishness. Paul squarely confronts that dilemma. His juxtaposition of both Jews and Greeks viewing the gospel's witness as folly is revealing. The Greeks were enamored of wisdom. And what wisdom resides in proclaiming a God who suffers? The Jews sought signs, a word rich in Old Testament associations with God's mighty works that brought freedom out of Egyptian bondage. Yet in the cross-formed theology of Paul, the chief sign of deliverance was not death unleashed against Egyptian firstborn to reveal God's power but death willingly endured by Mary's firstborn to reveal the depth of God's redemptive love.

Such proclamation was foolishness to the wisdom and power that held sway in Paul's day. And such proclamation remains foolish in the eyes of contemporary conventional wisdoms and their presumptions of power. *Might makes right. Those who have the most toys at the end win. You've got to go along to get along.* We can go on and on with the varied wisdoms and understandings of power that saturate how we conduct our affairs and organize our institutions—even our religious ones.

Paul describes the gospel as foolishness because when we proclaim its message rightly it does not conform to the conventional wisdoms and powers that hold sway in this world. Furthermore, Paul's words depict a rather unflattering portrayal of those whom God has chosen to proclaim this message because our job is not to beat those who view us as foolish. Rather, our job is to proclaim a radically different wisdom that intentionally puts us out of step with the prevailing norms. Our fool's errand is to proclaim the unsettling yet redemptive truth that what matters most in this world is what—and Who—transforms life for the good.

> *Recall the familiar courtroom oath: "Do you swear to tell the truth, the whole truth, and nothing but the truth?" Where have you experienced the gospel's proclamation cutting against the grain of prevailing opinion—including your own?*

DAY 2 • *Discerning the Season*

Read Jeremiah 1:9-10.

For everything there is a season, and a time for every matter under heaven." These familiar words from Ecclesiastes are often intoned in worship at times of passage or transition. But tucked beneath their assuring reflection on the rhythmic cycle of all things lies a disturbing truth. While everything has its season, not all that happens in this world and our lives comes seasonably:

- the untimely word spoken out of resentment or ignorance that cuts deeply or publicly

- the unseasonable deed that, in its haste or thoughtlessness, does not take into account its consequences for others

- the inopportune death, untimely for far more reasons than can be determined by the measure of a calendar

The time is never right for just anything to happen. Life and faith consider what is appropriate, what is timely, what is seasonable. The gospel's truth-telling requires discerning the season and context into which it is proclaimed lest the message be untimely, out of sync with that moment's particular need.

Consider Jeremiah's call. On the surface, it appears that God has muddied the waters for his young prophet with contradictory commands. We can imagine one retort from Jeremiah: *So just what is it you want me to do, God: tear down and destroy or build up and plant? Make a choice. You can't have it both ways.* We may sympathize with such a question. We prefer consistency and constancy. The gospel and its proclamation should be one way or the other—tearing down or building, destroying or planting—not a conglomeration of polar opposites.

The problem with that approach, in the wisdom of Ecclesiastes and Jeremiah's prophetic summons, is the seasonableness of all things. Life remains in constant flux. The context in which we proclaim the gospel plays a crucial role in the truths we tell at any given moment. Again, consider Jeremiah. To a people comfortable with life as it is, including striking indifference to justice and clinging to false hopes ("'Peace, peace,' when there is no peace," 6:14), the truth Jeremiah speaks is clear: pluck up and pull down, tear down and destroy. Yet, when Israel's context devolves into exile and descends into despair, the truth Jeremiah speaks is equally clear: to build and plant. "At that time, I will raise up a righteous branch from David's line, who will do what is just and right" (33:15, CEB).

The gospel's proclamation involves discerning the season so that we tell the truth that we and others need to hear rather than the truth we would prefer to hear or we hope will make people like us. Peter wanted to hear the truth of a warrior Messiah who would inflict suffering on enemies. Instead, Jesus told the truth about a Messiah who suffered, even for the sake of enemies.

What gospel truth do you most need to hear in this season of your life? Speak, Lord, your servant is listening.

DAY 3 • *From Ashes to Garlands*

Read Isaiah 61:1-3.

Anational menswear company sponsors an annual campaign to collect used suits and sport coats. Donors receive a coupon they can apply to a purchase. More importantly, the donated clothing is given to unemployed men for job interviews as they transition back into the workforce. "Clothes make the man" (or woman) is an old adage that we sometimes use to rationalize our overstuffed closets. However, the way we deck ourselves out may express our feelings about ourselves and how we want others to see us.

In the passage from Isaiah, the proclamation of Jubilee ("year of the Lord's favor") sets into motion a set of transformative actions. Oppressed ones receive good news. Brokenhearted ones experience a binding up of those breaks. Captives and prisoners find liberty and release. And returning to our opening paragraph's emphasis on clothing: God promises Israel in exile "a garland instead of ashes." Wait a minute! Ashes as clothing? And a garland? Isn't that an antiquated word to describe what our great-grandparents strung around preelectrified Christmas trees?

Context is everything. In the context of Isaiah's day, ashes and garlands relate to dress. Ashes and dust or ashes and sackcloth are images in scripture for the "clothing" donned in times of grief and mourning. In Jeremiah 6:26, the prophet bids the people to put on sackcloth and roll in ashes as exile approaches. Garland, in contrast, translates a Hebrew word for "headdress" or "ornament" or "turban." Such clothing belonged to times of celebration. "A garland instead of ashes" envisions a change in dress for Israel. But the cause for this change of clothing is not personal whim or fleeting styles. The cause is God's Jubilee that promises return from exile and restoration of land and hope.

Isaiah proclaims Jubilee and tells of its restorative truth to folks who have languished in the clothing of mourning. Garlands are not promised to folks already decked out in silks and custom-made finery. Isaiah proclaims garlands in place of ashes and the gospel's contemporary truth-telling of hope and joy in place of grief and despair to people who are all too familiar with being clothed in ashes.

Perhaps Jesus had these very words in mind when disciples wondered aloud about his words of imminent departure. "A little while, and you will no longer see me . . . you will have pain, but your pain will turn into joy" (John 16:19-20). From ashes to garlands, from pain to joy. Cross-formed proclamation does not minimize the difficult truths of our lives, but it speaks the truth of God's restorative power into those voids and beckons us to clothe ourselves with the gospel's transformative hope.

Be mindful of people who currently wear ashes. How can you be an agent of God's transformative hope in their lives?

DAY 4 • *Afflicting the Comfortable*

Read Matthew 23:23-24.

Years ago, I attended the installation service of a young pastor. The officiant proceeded routinely through the liturgy, including the traditional charge to "comfort the afflicted." But then he paused and added, "And afflict the comfortable." Laughter arose in the congregation, which I attributed to experience-borne recognition of that commission's unsettling truth. Proclaiming the gospel sometimes requires telling truths that disturb comfort zones for the sake of the gospel's transformative purposes.

A children's hymn written by Charles Wesley begins "gentle Jesus, meek and mild." The scribes and Pharisees would probably not describe Jesus as gentle, meek, or mild. Jesus' truth-telling to them issued indictments of "hypocrites" and "blind guides" in response to their scrupulousness in the tithing of herbs and their neglect in practicing justice and mercy. In a subsequent verse in that same passage, Jesus compares them to "white washed tombs," an image insinuating a false veneer of piety intended to disguise a deadened spirit within. Gentle Jesus, meek and mild? If we think Jesus told hard truths only to opponents, consider what he says elsewhere to Peter (*petros*), the "rock" upon whom he will build his church: "Get behind me, Satan!" (Matt. 16:23).

Jesus does not lash out for the sport of it or because the gospel has a mean streak to it. Jesus speaks hard truths for the sake of transformation: To transform the scribes' and Pharisees' comfy understanding of the law's demands by asserting the priorities of justice and mercy. To transform Peter by challenging the vision of a Messiah who inflicts suffering with the Messiah who will soon endure suffering.

The proclamation of the gospel still includes afflicting the comfortable. It is not the only aspect of the gospel's proclamation. But the more seductive option of the church in every age has been to avoid the affliction of the comfortable. Feel free to substitute any number of synonyms in place of "comfortable": powerful, privileged, contented. We avoid telling hard truths in those circumstances largely because we don't want to disturb comfort zones that get too close to home in our congregations or communities. The gospel's transformative purposes in terms of afflicting comfortable ones may be fine for others, but let's stay in the comfort business around here.

Except . . . except, as that young pastor was charged long ago and as Jesus embodied in his own ministry, the gospel's proclamation as truth-telling must indeed at times afflict the comfortable—even when ours is the status quo in need of such affliction.

What hard truth do you and your church need to speak and hear for the gospel's sake?

DAY 5 • *Bottom Lines*

Read Romans 8:31-39.

What then are we to say about these things?" Paul's opening question has as its trigger the "sufferings of this present time" (Rom. 8:18). Paul then goes on to catalogue those sufferings: hardship, distress, persecution, famine, nakedness, peril, sword.

What "sufferings of this present time" would evoke Paul's question today? A black youth shot down in a Cleveland park or a black pastor and parishioners whose hospitality at a prayer meeting was returned with a hail of gunfire? A culture of violence against women that only gets the public limelight when it threatens the unseemly profit margins of professional sports corporations? The hate-filled theologies of radical jihadists and white supremacists who share the goal of hammering plowshares into swords for the sake of imposing worldviews by threat of death? What then are we to say about *these* things?

In his cataloging of present sufferings, Paul does not deny their existence or minimize their impact on persons or communities. Rather, Paul responds that none of these things can separate us from the love of God in Jesus Christ. Paul's evidence for that assertion is the cross-illuminated witness of love expended for our sake. For Paul, it all comes down to what we make of the phrase "if God is for us." If God is for us, he argues, it does not matter who stands against us. The outcome is assured: Nothing will dethrone the power of love. Proclaiming the gospel is telling that truth, especially in the face of any and all "against us" claimants.

At this point, the gospel's proclamation faces a serious challenge. Nothing "will be able to separate us from the love of God in Christ" can devolve into a spiritual sedative that confuses faith with sitting back and idly waiting for God's sovereign realm while remaining pious bystanders to powers and principalities that inflict the "sufferings of this present time" (Rom. 8:18).

Gospel proclamation functions not as a sedative but as a stimulant. The truth that nothing "will be able to separate us" (Rom. 8:39) cries out to those who labor under the sufferings of this present time—and to the powers that impose those sufferings. The bottom line of God's advocacy provides us with the truth that will transform these times with the power of hope. Proclaiming that nothing "will be able to separate us" will not defang all would-be rivals to the ultimate power of God's love, but we should not assume that we can do or say nothing in the face of this time's present sufferings.

We can.

We can tell and live the truth that nothing will be able to separate us from God's love. Any claim or claimant to the contrary will not stand.

"If God is for us . . ." Do you believe that? If so, how and to whom might you tell and live its truth?

DAY 6 • *Simplicity and Transformation*

Read John 19:28.

I am thirsty." Of all the so-called seven last words of Jesus, these may be the most rudimentary. Set aside for a moment the varied theologies of atonement or God's coming realm that complicate our interpretations of what it means to forgive and be forgiven or to promise remembrance to a dying thief. Listen in utter simplicity to the truth Jesus tells in that moment in these words.

"I am thirsty."

Some might ask, Where is the gospel proclamation in that? Isn't Jesus simply blurting out what he feels and nothing more? The truth is, Jesus is blurting out what he feels—and nothing less! To unleash the possibility of transformation, the gospel's proclamation must begin with what is felt as most true and pressing in any given moment. That aspect gives the Sunday morning context of proclamation its enormous potential. Pulpited words should express what is most true and most pressing in the lives of worshipers and in the life of the world into which God sends those congregants to serve.

Through the simplicity of these words on the cross, Jesus proclaims the gospel truth. Or, to be more specific, Jesus proclaims two gospel truths. The first truth is one the church has wrestled with since its inception: the truth of Jesus' humanity. "I am thirsty" cannot be honestly spoken by one who is only divine. Jesus is not "above it all" on the cross, merely appearing to undergo its suffering. Jesus knows and experiences human existence from the inside out. "I am thirsty" proclaims the truth rendered in one contemporary statement of faith in this way: "God has come to us and shared our common lot."

The other more subtle but equally compelling truth proclaimed in "I am thirsty" is this: The gospel always awaits faithful response. Jesus' thirst admits a need that another must meet. Unless he conjures up a glass of water, Jesus is in no position to assuage his most pressing need in that moment. All he can do is cry out in thirst. While interpreters may disagree over motive, John's Gospel describes what follows: The guards beneath the cross respond by providing something to drink.

In the end, is that not the goal of all gospel proclamation and truth-telling: to evoke response to what is most pressing, whether for our lives or for others, in hopes of transformation? For the soldiers, "I am thirsty" invites them to shift from executioners to ministers. And for us? Jesus' simplicity in proclaiming "I am thirsty" beckons us to tell the pressing truths about ourselves and those around us in order to enable a response that embodies the gospel's transformative possibilities revealed in light of the cross.

Holy God, you promise life-giving water to all who thirst. May I drink and channel its gift. Amen.

WEEK FIVE

Creed: Owning the Faith

You may own the faith every Sunday or only occasionally. You may do so using the words of one of the church's classical creeds (Apostles' Creed, Nicene Creed) or a statement framed by your denomination. In any case, you have likely had the experience of offering an affirmation of faith in company with a gathered congregation.

But what are you doing in that act? You are affirming your personal allegiance to the God. You are setting the stage for putting your faith into action beyond the safe confines of sanctuary. And you are not doing so in isolation. You are owning words and faith that have come down to you from community: the one with whom you gather, to be sure; but equally important, as one creed speaks of it, with the "communion of saints" spread over place and time and circumstance. Your claim and ensuing embodiment of this faith to which you testify as your own is critical. But owning the faith is always communal. "I believe" grows out of and melds into "we believe."

This week's readings will explore how we see most fully the marks and consequences of owning the faith in light of the cross. For whether the context is worship or discipleship, the faith we own connects our way to the way owned by the crucified and risen Christ.

DAY 1 • *Follow-Through*

Read Luke 23:33-34.

In sports, *follow-through* has to do with the continuation of motion after a ball has been thrown or struck. A pitcher does not stop moving arm and legs as soon as the ball leaves the hand, nor does a batter stop the swing at the moment of impact. To do so would greatly reduce the force and direction of the ball, not to mention increasing the risk of injury to the body. Follow-through entails more than a graceful ending to a pitch or hit. It is a necessary component in accomplishing what the player has set out to do.

Follow-through is essential in all manner of human endeavors. If you make a promise, speaking the promissory word alone is not enough. You need to follow through. If you start a project, gathering the resources and initiating the task is not enough, no matter how good or encouraging the start. You need to follow through.

So it should not surprise us that Christian discipleship requires follow-through. Owning the faith does not end with the recitation of a creedal summary of our beliefs in worship. Owning the faith comes in following through on those beliefs in the conduct of our daily lives.

Consider today's reading. Throughout his life and ministry, Jesus reveals his beliefs about forgiveness. In what we have come to call the Lord's Prayer, Jesus asserts his belief that our forgiveness by God is inextricably woven into our forgiving of others ("forgive us our debts, as we also have forgiven our debtors" [Matt. 6:12]). Jesus reinforces that belief when Peter asks how many times he must forgive someone who sins against him. The gist of Jesus' answer in the ensuing parable, beyond

Week Five 73

the "seventy times seven" (Matt. 18:22, footnote), condemns a servant who is forgiven an incredible debt but who then refuses to forgive another of a comparatively minor liability. In other narratives, Jesus announces forgiveness to many folks.

Jesus' words about forgiveness are all well and good. Cynics could protest that Jesus' bestowing forgiveness on others (such as a woman caught in adultery) or his teaching of forgiveness never involved his forgiving someone who trespassed on his turf. Forgiving others as an uninvolved third party proves nothing. Will Jesus forgive when push comes to shove in his own life? Will Jesus follow through and own the faith he has taught when another causes him pain?

When nails are driven, when crossbar is hoisted, when executioners do unholy work, when taunters gather to mock, Jesus says, "Father, forgive them; for they know not what they do" (KJV). Jesus aimed at forgiveness, and his motion continues after the moment of cross-imposed impact in gracious follow-through. He owns his faith.

Where, O God, do I need to follow through in the faith and forgiveness you would set into motion in and through my life? Amen.

DAY 2 • *Who(se) We Are*

Read Deuteronomy 26:5-9.

We do not always find it easy or comfortable to own some parts of who we are. However, avoiding such admission—such *owning*—of all that encompasses our identity results in blind spots or festering wounds. For example, some would avoid not owning the racism that still runs deep in this nation, preferring to think that civil rights legislation or the election of President Barack Obama ended it. We cannot wish things like racism and income inequality away simply by denial or under a haze of Pollyanna-ish rhetoric. They are part of who we are. The challenge comes in owning such components of our identity, whether personal or national, for the sake of finding a way that brings redemptive transformation to the role they play in our lives.

I once heard Deuteronomy described as "the gospel according to Moses." The book contains much good news: the gift of Torah, the promise of a land flowing with milk and honey. Deuteronomy even shapes the gospel proclaimed by Jesus. When a lawyer comes asking about the law's greatest commandment, Jesus draws his answer from Deuteronomy 6:5, "You shall love the LORD your God with all your heart, and with all your soul, and with all your might." (See Matthew 22:35-37.)

Deuteronomy also contains one of the earliest confessions of faith in the Old Testament set in a liturgy that dedicates the offerings of the first fruits of harvest. Amazingly, *crucially*, this foundational creed of Israel begins not with who God is but who we are. "A wandering Aramean was my ancestor; he went down into Egypt and lived there as an alien" (26:5). Who are the Israelites? Landless wanderers. Once they cross into Egypt, they are "illegal" immigrants. Israel's owning of faith does not begin in an honorific listing of all the *right* people. Israel's "who we are" of faith begins with no one of account. Israel's creedal owning of faith makes clear that the ensuing narrative of deliverance owes to God's grace and not their pedigree.

So it is for us. Faith asks us to own who we are, which is not always who we pretend we are. Otherwise, we would not so much need God's grace as God's congratulation. Owning who we are allows God's transformative purposes to work on all that comprises our identity, including those aspects that cause us and others grief. In doing so, such ownership opens us to the grace-filled possibilities of *whose* we are: those whom God seeks in cross-formed love to save.

Paraphrase Deuteronomy 26:5-9 according to your life's narrative of who and whose you are.

DAY 3 • *An Astonishing Thing*

Read John 9:24-34.

In the movie *The Shawshank Redemption*, the inmate Andy Dufresne comes to the warden with wonderful news. Andy has met an inmate who can identify the man who committed the murder for which Andy had been wrongfully convicted. The warden, however, has no desire to free Andy, whose book-keeping skills have been utilized by the warden to hide monies he has been embezzling. So the warden dismisses each of Andy's arguments for pursuing the matter. An exasperated Andy finally blurts out: "How can you be so obtuse?" The warden responds by placing Andy in solitary confinement, isolated from even the limited community afforded to convicts.

On the sabbath Jesus heals a man born blind, a man who quickly disappears from the scene. Some religious authorities who have already clashed with Jesus decide to question the newly sighted individual. The interrogation rapidly becomes a confrontation. The back and forth gets heated, particularly when the interrogators assert they follow Moses but have no idea where this Jesus comes from. John records the healed one's response as "here is an astonishing thing!"—which is basically Andy's "how can you be so obtuse?" The one who can now see takes these religious authorities to task for the obtuseness of not wanting to admit the origin of such power to heal. Ironically, these authorities react as does the Shawshank warden: They separate the man who now sees from the community—"they drive him out."

What distinguishes the insight of the man born blind is his willingness to own the faith he has just experienced in the healing touch of Jesus. His "creed" is the experience of his healing that convinces him of the God-grounded origin of the One who brought sight to his life. He may not know the details and intricacies of Torah that the Pharisees have gained through years of study. But he has come to know two things from the inside out. The first is, "that though I was blind, now I see" (John 9:25). The second is, "If this man were not from God, he could do nothing" (John 9:33). He affirms that belief, even though it costs him community.

We may read this text and go no farther than astonishment at how those leaders could be so could be so obtuse. But that would be a mistake born of self-righteousness. The more trans-forming astonishment comes when we allow the text to ask what faith we own, even and especially when it comes at cost. Like the man born blind who now sees, what do we know and what faith do we confess that cuts to the core of who we are by the grace of God?

Reflect on the whole of your spiritual journey. On what bedrock principles do you ground your faith? How does your daily life own those principles?

DAY 4 • *We Shall Not Fear*

Read Psalm 46.

Contrary to the frequent biblical admonition of "be not afraid," we live in an age and culture that implicitly and often explicitly encourages us to fear. The threat of "stranger danger" has become a mantra for warning our children in hopes of keeping them safe, in spite of the unsettling truth that family and friends are more likely to be abusers than strangers. We have grown accustomed to "terrorism alert" levels that jack up our fears. Much political rhetoric promotes fear-mongering, whether in the name of border security or gun rights. Be afraid, we are told, be very afraid, while those in the fear-provoking business rake in the profits.

Biblical faith strikes a different chord. Time and again the invitation "do not be afraid" precedes the good news of God's purposes. To Abram, when God brings the gift of covenant (Genesis 15:1); to Mary, when Gabriel announces God's favor (Luke 1:30); to shepherds, when the shining of God's glory terrifies them (Luke 2:9-10): To all these and more, the invitation is the same. Do not be afraid! Do not fear!

We could argue that this invitation is little more than whistling in the dark. We could perceive living without fear as a denial of life's realities. Only those with power, wealth, or good luck can possibly claim to live without fear. But even those people live with the fear of losing the things that insulate them. Power and wealth and luck run out at death, if not long before.

Scripture and the faith it evokes, however, do not live in denial. Psalm 46 acknowledges a host of fear-inducing troubles in its litany of natural upheavals. It is a list akin to Paul's later catalogue of experiences that could threaten to separate us from God (Romans 8:35). But while the psalmist and Paul affirm multiple reasons and experiences that give rise to fear, an all-embracing experience bids us not be afraid: God's presence. "God is our refuge," the psalmist declares—not once but three times. God is with us. For that reason—and not because we own a rapid-fire gun and not because we can seal our borders and not because we can isolate ourselves from strangers—we will not fear.

By owning such faith we find the means to live such a life. Experiences will trouble our lives and disrupt our world, but we shall not fear because God is with us in the midst of them.

What is your greatest fear? In what ways might "God is with us" move you toward owning "I will not fear"?

DAY 5 • *Compelled*

Read Acts 4:13-20.

On September 14, 2001, three days after the 9/11 attack, Congress approved the "Authorization for Use of Military Force against Terrorists" resolution by a vote of 420 to 1 (the remaining 14 members either were not present or did not vote). Congresswoman Barbara Lee cast the only no vote. She prefaced her speech on the house floor that day, which laid out the grounds for her opposition, with these words: "This unspeakable attack on the United States has forced me to rely on my moral compass, my conscience, and my God for direction." In the face of public censure and death threats, Congresswoman Lee owned her convictions. We cannot always go along to get along.

Peter and John stand before the Sanhedrin of Jerusalem. The council faces a difficult decision. Their annoyance at the preaching of these two has led to the apostles' arrest the prior day. But the populace perceives a healing by these two that same day as a "notable sign." Perhaps the Sanhedrin can reach a compromise: Peter and John's release in exchange for silencing their teaching and preaching in Christ's name. Peter and John reply, "Whether it is right in God's sight to listen to you rather than to God, you must judge; for we cannot keep from speaking about what we have seen and heard" (Acts 4:19-20). Peter and John own their faith. We cannot always go along to get along.

Both of these encounters share a common dynamic: being compelled to act based on what we hold to be true. When we affirm a faith statement or creed, we are not going through frivolous motions. The role of creeds in worship is to remind us of what we believe to be fundamentally true about God, the world, and our relationship to both. Creeds convey the basis of the way we conduct our lives and shape our priorities outside the confines of worship. Creeds set the framework for what initiates our actions and responses as disciples, particularly when it comes to choices that tempt us to exchange costly conviction for the lesser gods of expediency and appeasement.

Faith that is owned may compel us to do otherwise.

Ask Peter and John.

Ask Barbara Lee.

Ask Jesus on the cross.

What has faith compelled you to do? What does its compulsion seek of you now?

DAY 6 • *Renunciation*

Read Mark 15:29-32.

We tend to think of owning faith in exclusively positive terms: in the *yes* that confirms God's call, in the "We believe" that prefaces our testimonies of faith. The creeds themselves stylistically reflect the dominance of positive statements that express the tenets we confess as our own.

But another form of owning the faith comes primarily in renunciation, of saying *no* to whatever would betray or usurp God's claim upon our lives and creation.

Some liturgies of baptism reflect such owning by renunciation. It typically occurs at the outset of the opening questions posed to candidates or their sponsors: "Do you renounce the powers of evil?" Or, in the more ancient terms remembered in the liturgy of the Roman Catholic Church: "Do you reject Satan . . . and all his works . . . and all his empty promises?"

A crowd gathers at Golgotha to scoff at the crucified ones. Mark reveals that the mocking takes on particular venom when directed at Jesus. It is not simply that people twist Jesus' words about rebuilding the Temple. It is not simply that they sarcastically mouth the title of "Messiah" in his direction, a title that Jesus has resisted throughout Mark's Gospel. More significantly, they pose a test to the one dying before their eyes. If you really are who you or others say you are, come down off the cross. Save yourself. Make it about yourself.

In some ways, their taunt poses no new test for Jesus. It is the same test that the tempter posed in the wilderness at the outset of Jesus' ministry: Fling yourself off the Temple wall; God's angels will save you from harm. (See Matthew 4:5-7.) Peter posed the same test when rebuking Jesus after Peter's confession of "You are the Messiah." Jesus speaks of a Messiah who is rejected and suffers and is killed. (See Mark 8:31-32.) Jesus refuses the tempter's offer and rejects Peter's twisting of messianic purpose.

But now, at the last, comes yet another test. Come down off the cross. Save yourself. Make it about yourself.

The conventional wisdom of "living to fight another day" would argue in favor of coming down. But a deeper purpose is at work here than personal survival. Jesus' owning the Messiah he has come to be requires that he now renounce the Messiah that others taunt him to become. On the cross, faith comes embodied in an unspoken but unmistakable *no* that renounces the belief that saving begins and ends with self. Saving begins and ends with love revealed in light of the cross.

Holy God, what no *would you have me speak and act that would own the faith to which you call me today?*

WEEK SIX

Response: Stepping Out

Joshua 3:13 includes an intriguing detail about Israel's entry into the Promised Land. The people will have to cross the waters of the Jordan. God promises to part those waters, akin to God's parting of the sea when the Hebrews escaped Egypt. However, there is a catch. The Jordan's waters will part only when the priests bearing the ark step into the water. They cannot wait until all is dry and firm and certain. They have to get their feet wet and trust that a way will be made. They must step out in faith.

It is one thing to enter worship and revel in the gifts of word and sacrament that promise God's grace. It is quite another to step out of the sanctuary into the often chaotic waters of our lives, trusting in grace to make a way forward long before that way is clear. But like the Hebrews of old, we too have to get our feet wet first. Faith summons us to step out in faith.

The light and shadows cast by the Cross convey the risk of that response. Faithful response summons us to step into the water and, in doing so, trust the grace of God more than we fear the currents.

DAY 1 • *Taking the Point*

Read Mark 10:32-34.

Taking the point is a phrase often associated with the military tactic of an individual or small group advancing ahead of a larger unit. When traversing unknown territory, the point may function as a scout who finds the best route for others to follow. When traversing hostile territory, the point is the most exposed position, most likely to draw fire from an enemy so the larger group can avoid ambush. The experience of the one(s) who takes the point helps those who follow anticipate what lies in store for them.

Prior to Mark 8, the geographical movements of Jesus and the disciples seem rather random. They go here and there, back and forth, primarily in Galilee with no singular direction. That sense of random travel changes in chapter 8. Peter confesses Jesus to be the Christ, and Jesus consequently sets the unswerving direction for the Gospel's remaining chapters with the first of three passion predictions. No more meandering through the countryside. The journey moves in a decisive fashion both geographically and theologically toward Jerusalem.

In today's narrative from Mark, Jesus takes the point on the journey: "Jesus was walking ahead of them." That goes beyond a merely physical description of Jesus' location in proximity to the disciples. By taking the point, Jesus exposes himself to what lies ahead. By taking the point, Jesus reveals what may lie in store for those who follow. Mark relates that those who follow Jesus are afraid. Do they ground their fear in what Jesus has already said, not once but twice, about what will happen to him in Jerusalem? Do they ground their fear in what Jesus has said after the first passion prediction about his followers needing to take up their own cross? Or do they ground their fear in something from both?

The way is set. Jesus takes the point, and the response of discipleship then and now involves following the One whom Peter confessed as Christ. Faith does not consist of setting anchor in the safe harbor of liturgical or congregational cocoons, waiting for the storms of life to pass before we step out into the glory of unadulterated light. In Mark, Jesus takes the point amid gathering shadows and invites disciples to follow.

Consequently, the church's evangelical identity as the body of Christ asks us take the point for the sake of others who would follow today. Evangelism demonstrates the faith we hold by the lives we lead for the purpose of enabling others to follow Jesus. Likewise, worship formed by the cross inevitably leads to our stepping out in faithful response as Jesus did before us.

What would taking the point involve in terms of word and action in your faithful response to God for the sake of others who would follow?

DAY 2 • *Go Where I Send Thee*

Read Genesis 12:1-4.

Perhaps you are familiar with the spiritual whose title heads this reading. It is a "counting" song whose lyrics gradually build on being sent "one by one," "two by two," until the final number (anywhere from eight to thirteen) is reached. But whatever the version and whatever characters are used for the counting ("one for the little bitty baby, two for Paul and Silas"), one feature remains constant, "Go where I send thee."

While the stories of Creation and Fall, flood and rainbow come first, the Abraham and Sarah narratives have taken precedence over them as the foundational stories for Jewish and Christian identity. Judaism speaks not of Father Adam but Father Abraham. When Paul weaves his theology of faith's preeminence in Romans 4 and Galatians 3, the exemplar is Abraham. And where does the narrative of Abraham and Sarah begin? "Go . . . to the land that [God] will show you." In other words, go where I send thee.

Faith for Abraham and Sarah does not begin in accepting traditioned doctrinal theses or affirming particular tenets of scriptural authority. Faith literally begins by stepping out in response to God's summons. And lest we think of faith's response as a cakewalk, so to speak, it is important to remember that the act of stepping *out* in one direction always entails stepping *away* from others. Consider the call given to Abraham and Sarah. The "go to" in verse 1 is preceded by what they are called to "go from": land ("country") and family ("kindred"). Given that the narrator of Genesis has already disclosed Sarah's barrenness (11:30), we could ask, what is left? They set out, leaving all that provides security in their culture. Without land, without ancestral family, and at this point without descendants: Where will these two place their hope if they choose to go where God sends? They will place it in the promissory nature of God: "I will make of you . . . I will bless you."

Notice God's verb tense there: "I *will.*" The promises joined to "go" are future tense. The decision Abraham and Sarah make about going or not going takes place in the prolonged "not yet" between present summons and future fulfillment. Faith does not wait to set out until all the answers are in and all the doubts are settled. If that were the case, faith would not be faith but foregone conclusion.

Children, go where I send thee.

Where, O God, would you send me and what will that journey ask me to leave behind? Amen.

DAY 3 • *Not in My Backyard*

Read Amos 7:12-15.

Perhaps you have encountered the acronym NIMBY: Not In My Backyard. For example, we easily admit the need for halfway houses to reorient felons into community life. But putting such a place on the same block as your home? Not in my backyard! We also hear such objections when outsiders threaten to disrupt our places of living, whether neighborhoods or ways of life or religion.

So it was for Amos of Judah. God may have called him to be a prophet, but that message encountered a wall at the border of Israel and Judah. When Amos steps out in response to God's call and brings his "thus says the LORD" into the northern kingdom of Israel, Amaziah, the court prophet of the northern kingdom reacts, "O seer, go, flee away to the land of Judah, earn your bread there, and prophesy there; but never again prophesy at Bethel, for it is the king's sanctuary" (Amos 7:12-13). In other words: not in my backyard.

Amaziah's resistance to an outsider disturbing his home-land is by no means unique to the eighth century BCE. When I wrote this, it had only been two weeks since a jihadist couple went on a shooting rampage in San Bernardino, California. In the immediate aftermath of that tragic event, more than two-thirds of one presidential candidate's supporters endorsed demands ranging from banning Muslims' entry into this country to creating a national registry for those already here. And of all those raising a cry against these "outsiders," few urged similar interdictions against Christian antiabortion activists in wake of the shooting rampage at the Planned Parenthood office in Colorado Springs barely a week before. Apparently, aversion to murder carried out in the name of perversions of religion differs on the basis of whether the killers are "ours" or "theirs." The spirit of Amaziah remains alive and well when fear condemns the "other" among us even as it avoids hard truths that fall too close to home.

Amaziah wished to rid his country and king—his backyard—of this troublesome outsider named Amos. But the terms *outsiders* and *insiders* carry little weight when it comes to God's call to step out in faith. Worship formed in light of the cross recognizes that call may necessitate precarious stepping out from the safety of sanctuary and home in order to bring the word of God's judgment and grace to wherever and upon whomever it falls. Amos could have remained a herdsman in Judah. Instead, he stepped out in faithful response. Amaziah could have reexamined his prophetic call in Israel. Instead, he blocked out God's call by closing the door on Amos—and, as it turned out, by closing the door on Israel's last hope for turning.

> *O God, where and to whom will you send me—and whose disruptive word in my life might call me to renewal?*

DAY 4 • *Fieldwork*

Read John 21:15-17.

The seminary I attended required every student preparing for pastoral ministry to combine each semester's academic work with at least ten hours a week of what was called fieldwork, practical experience in a ministry setting. The term *field* has its origins in a far more agrarian culture than that evidenced in Webster Groves in the 1970s. Perhaps the seminary could have employed a more modern term to describe the setting for ministry in the latter quarter of twentieth-century America.

However, fieldwork connects directly with another word that describes the vocation for which this experience would prepare us: *pastor. Pastorum* comes from the Latin word for shepherd, and its verb form *pastere* means "to lead to pasture, . . . cause to eat." *Pastor* clearly draws on shepherding imagery. The Bible strongly links that imagery with leadership in and care of community.

Today's episode from John's Gospel draws on those associations in its story of Jesus commissioning Peter. The setting is post-Resurrection, the interim period between Jesus' having been raised and his ascension. That timing suggests a season of preparation—Jesus readying disciples to be sent out into the world in the face of his imminent departure. The threefold structure of Jesus' questions and commissions calls to mind Peter's earlier threefold denial. Before Peter can set out in faithful response on the road ahead, he must clear the way of a guilt-crippling past. Three times, Jesus follows his question of "do you love me" with variations on a shepherd's central task: feeding and tending lambs and sheep. Fieldwork. More specifically, fieldwork identified as nurturing those entrusted to Peter's care. Peter, the "rock" (*petros*) upon whom Jesus will build the church, is the person to whom Jesus elsewhere entrusts the "keys of the kingdom." Peter will fulfill his calling by working in the field with vulnerable and hungry ones entrusted to his care. And by way of Peter, they are the ones entrusted to our care.

Every time we step out of worship, we step into the vocation entrusted to Peter, the fieldwork of loving those beloved by God. What brings a cross-formed edge to such love is the last phrase of the preceding sentence: *loving those beloved by God.* We will love those who may not be beloved by us. Our fieldwork of care does not differentiate between those whom we deem to deserve the love of God and those whom we do not. Jesus established the breadth of God's love on the cross.

This is not pew work, accomplished in the safety of sanctuaries. This is fieldwork, where love responds to human need in daily acts of grace, justice, and compassion.

Look around you. Who within your reach needs feeding and tending? What one act will you take this week that carries shepherding love into the field?

DAY 5 • *Disturbers of the Peace*

Read Matthew 21:12-15.

Yesterday's disturbers of the peace may be lauded as today's role models. Consider these remarks offered by Jeh C. Johnson, Secretary of the Department of Homeland Security, at the Martin Luther King Jr. memorial on January 20, 2015:

> The reality is that, in his time, the man we honor today with a national holiday was divisive; to many, he was a trouble-maker, to force the social change we now all celebrate. He challenged the social order of things and pushed people out of their comfort zones.

From a distance, we may tolerate and even honor faraway disturbers of the peace—so long as it is not our peace that gets disturbed. The account of Jesus disrupting business-as-usual commerce at the Temple is a case in point. From a distance, we cheer as tables get turned on currency exchangers and sellers of animals. But put yourself in the place of those disrupted entre-preneurs. Money changers are there because the half-shekel Temple tax needs to be paid with a particular local coin rather than currencies brought by pilgrims from far and wide. Like-wise, the sellers of animals are there because the law required unblemished animals for sacrifice. Traveling any significant dis-tance with such animals would have slowed the journey and made the trip more expensive.

Both money changers and sellers provide a needed service for pilgrims who have traveled to worship at the Temple. To exchange money or sell animals at cost would have left the vendors unable to support their own families. So how would you have reacted to Jesus disturbing your peace and livelihood?

Would you have lobbied for Jesus' recognition as Messiah or for his condemnation as an uncivil troublemaker?

The example of Jesus in the Temple unsettles because it implies some faithful responses will *not* receive public acclaim. Sometimes our stepping into discipleship will demand words and actions that disturb status quos—including ones we cherish, including ones embedded in our religious communities. Dr. King's now-acclaimed *Letter from a Birmingham Jail* voiced his response to a published statement by local clergy that avowed their support for civil rights but considered Dr. King's tactics to be "unwise and untimely." Unwise and untimely. We may wonder if such an assessment clouds our view of actions that appear unseemly in this moment but that future generations will honor as faithful.

Both Mark and Luke record the following response to Jesus' actions at the Temple: "[They] kept looking for a way to kill him." Ironically, authorities arrested Dr. King and placed him in the Birmingham jail on April 12, 1963: Good Friday. The cross forms our response to God's call—and sometimes its consequences.

> *What peace in your community or church may need disturbing for the gospel's sake? What will you do— and risk—in faithful response?*

DAY 6 • *Entrusting Self to God*

Read Luke 23:46.

"Let go and let God." I carry a great deal of ambivalence about that expression. At times persons speak those words to abdicate personal responsibility. I once was part of a group from St. Louis that attended a Christian conference for youth and young adults in Dallas. Most of us had made arrangements for housing and meals during our travels and stay. But one man proudly informed us at the final planning meeting that he had made no such arrangements. He trusted that God would provide all he needed. To me, his letting go and letting God seemed at best an artificial testing of God—and at worst, an egotistical imposition of his needs on others.

On the other hand, life does confront us with experiences where we must let go of personal control and entrust the situation to another. People who go into surgery under general anesthesia understand that they can do nothing other than let go and entrust themselves to the hands of the surgical team. In a related way, parents come to junctures when they must let go and trust the children they have raised to live as responsible and independent adults.

Today's verse from Luke concerns a pivotal moment of letting go in Jesus' life. At this point, he has no more parables to tell, no more healings to accomplish, no more roads to take. All that remains before Jesus is death. He could have bargained for just one more day. He could have lashed out at those who crucified him. He could have refused to accept the inevitable. Instead, Jesus accepted it as a moment of letting go: not in a despairing resignation bereft of hope but in a strongly voiced trust of the One who had confirmed Jesus at baptism as

Beloved of God. "Into your hands I commend my spirit." With such trust, Jesus enters death.

Jesus' entrusting of self into God's hands models for us a practice of stepping out in faithful response on discipleship's path. Such letting go as Jesus demonstrates need not wait for the time of our dying, although it surely may accompany us there as well. Entrusting ourselves into God's hands guides our entry into every day and each encounter throughout. We do not confuse entrusting ourselves to God with flight from appropriate responsibility. Rather, entrusting ourselves into God's hands becomes the unreserved offering of who we are and what we have into every God-given and God-graced possibility.

"Into your hands I commend my spirit." What would it mean for you to live out these words today?

HOLY WEEK

Sacrament: Recognizing God

Somewhere along the line, most likely in confirmation, I came across the following understanding of *sacrament*: "the visible sign of an invisible grace." Like many subjects in Jesus' parables, those visible signs in the church's sacramental practice take form and substance in the most ordinary elements: water, bread, wine, juice. The routine and common convey God's grace to us.

Holy Week may seem anything but routine or common. The hymn "Were You There" justifiably evokes awe-filled reflection on this week's cross-shaped core in its haunting line of "sometimes it causes me to tremble." Yet the events recalled this week with such awe are grounded in universal experiences of human existence: the fellowship of table, the pain of death, the uncertainty of grieving, the joy of reunion. All these are common experiences, visible signs of what it means to be human. And in this week, each one takes on sacramental meaning. For whether at table or in death, through vigil or in joy, God's invisible grace comes to the fore and elicits our recognition of the Holy One's presence in our midst.

Faith challenges us to recognize God's unseen grace in life's most common of experiences and companions. "Sacrament" as the final movement in worship formed in light of the cross reminds us that sacramental observances in worship are, in their purpose, liturgical preparations for opening our eyes to see the Holy One whose presence we may encounter in the common and routine of life.

Foretaste
(Maundy Thursday)

Read Matthew 26:26-30.

Tasting rooms" are almost a requirement these days for commercial vineyards. Samples of wine are offered, not simply to stimulate the palate but to instill the desire to purchase that bottle (or case!) for enjoyment on some future occasion. A similar stratagem is at work in neighborhood or city-wide events often called "A Taste of . . . " where local restaurants provide samplings of their dishes. There too the restaurateurs hope that tasting the house specialties will result in a visit by those customers to their eatery. *Foretaste* rightly identifies the function of such small samplings to stir anticipation of what will later be experienced more fully.

Maundy Thursday commemorates Jesus' gathering with the disciples at table one final time before the cross. The sacrament of Communion summons the church's remembrance of that table. But such recollection dare not limit itself to looking back. "Take, eat" and "drink from it" are not Jesus' only words at that table. After the tasting comes the foretaste. "I will never again drink of this fruit of the vine until that day when I drink it new with you in my Father's kingdom." Remembrance and anticipation inseparably join in this meal and in its grace.

Jesus provides several foretastes here. "Never again" instills the flavor of tension and grieving that saturate Jesus' expressed expectations at this table. Change and upheaval are about to be unleashed: It will not be easy, and it will not leave Jesus unscathed. "Never again" imparts a taste of apprehension to this table, then and now. But "never again" is not the last word. "Until that day when I drink it new" injects a radical foretaste of hope into Jesus' expectations. Even in the impending change and upheaval, even in the scathing and wounding and dying that loom, Jesus affirms the anticipation of restored relationship.

Jesus gives expression to a third foretaste, one that draws us directly into the drama, by affirming that hope and restoration are not solely his nor those first disciples': "until that day when I drink it new with you." *With you.* In gathering at this table, we do not simply remember what was said and done two millennia ago. We anticipate what will endure for all millennia to come. In this table's bits of bread and sips of juice, we sample and recognize God's gracious foretaste of restoration with Christ and the whole of God's people. This expectation can sustain us in hope, especially when for us—as for Jesus at that table—what looms ahead will not be easy, including the drawing near of death itself.

Do this in remembrance of me.

Do this in hope of me.

The next time you celebrate Communion, anticipate in these elements the foretaste of hope. Consider how this foretaste can transform what you will do and who you will be this day.

He Descended into Hell
(Good Friday)

Read Mark 15:6-37.

So the traditional wording of the Apostles' Creed confesses Jesus' whereabouts in the time between death and raising, as alluded to in the assertion of 1 Peter 3:18-19. In the creed, this phrase follows "he was crucified, died, and was buried." But let me suggest it would be equally true if we reversed the order of those two articles in the creed. The descent into hell does not wait for Good Friday's climax in death. Rather, the tortuous slide begins in the hell-on-earth injustice and humiliation that open this day.

Mark narrates that descent in brutal clarity. Pilate abdicates justice-rendering authority to the whims of the crowd, freeing a convicted murderer and condemning an innocent teacher. Soldiers inaugurate Golgotha's violent humiliation by flogging and spitting on Jesus while offering mock allegiance to a king whose head they crown with thorns. And after driving nails and hoisting the victim into the air for a slow-motion execution, the guards gamble for clothes unceremoniously stripped off his body. Unlike in Luke, no defense of Jesus arises from one of the thieves crucified with him. In Mark, Jesus' companions in crucifixion lend their voices to the taunters and mockers. Unlike in John, no mother and beloved disciple wait at the foot of the cross for Jesus to confer a blessing of new familial relationship. In Mark, the only ones who witness Jesus' agony up close and personal are executioners and enemies. Hell on earth most aptly describes this seemingly God-forsaken place, as Jesus' own cry of *Eloi, eloi, lema sabachthani* would appear to attest: *My God, my God, why have you forsaken me?*

But that very cry of forsakenness reveals something other than hell-on-earth. In absolute forsakenness, with God nowhere to be found, the cry would make no sense as it never could be heard. All should then be silence. But Jesus is not silent. Even on this hell-hill, God can be encountered—if only for the moment in lament.

Good Friday contains, in the terms of this week's emphasis, sacramental possibility: the possibility of recognizing the presence of God even in the worst of circumstances. Do not take this to mean that all that happens to Jesus on this day is good and part of God's will. Quite the opposite. Rather, it means that powers and events laden with evil, bent on bringing hell on earth, cannot banish God. The gospel formed by the cross declares that when we descend into such times, God does not abandon us. We are not lost to God. We belong to God.

On Good Friday, the powers of death have done their worst. But their worst threat cannot undo God's enduring promise: I am with you. I will be with you.

On this Good Friday, where do you discern God's presence and hope in your experiences of suffering?

Sabbath Vigil
(Holy Saturday)

Read Luke 23:55-56.

Holy Saturday awkwardly interrupts the church's calendar. We read in Luke of the women who rest on this day in sabbath observance. But we find it hard to replicate their rest in our day. The prior week's preparations for palm processions, passion week cantatas, and/or seven last word recollections leave little time for decorating sanctuaries and making ready for Easter breakfasts and final practices of brass quartets for Sunday's alleluias—not to mention eggs to dye and family banquets to prepare. So much to do on Saturday and so little time.

But Holy Saturday offers this advice to activist-bent individuals and congregations and denominations like my own: *Don't just do something, stand there.* Sometimes, our busyness cocoons and insulates us from deep consideration of why we think our lives require constant motion. Busyness has often been a prescription for overcoming grief. Do this, do that, work your way out of it. But once the activity dies down, when exhaustion inevitably sets in, the questions and the pain remain, perhaps aggravated by delay in their contemplation.

The women in Luke actively engage in the immediate aftermath of crucifixion. They follow to see where the body has been taken. They prepare spices and ointments for anointing the corpse. But instead of pressing ahead in a rush to get things done ASAP: They stop. They keep sabbath. In Luke's terms, they rest. Luke's word *heschazo* carries dual meanings of "to keep quiet" and "to cease from labor." The women keep Saturday's vigil in stillness and quietness.

Does rest provide an escape from responsibilities in the wake of what has happened? Or does it offer an opportunity to contemplate and struggle for acceptance of what has happened? Luke does not answer those questions for us. He simply relates that the women's sabbath vigil is one of rest.

And what of us? What vigil do we keep in the aftermath of Good Friday? The women's restful vigil did not benefit from hindsight, of knowing that tomorrow stones will be rolled away and lilies will bedeck chancels. Do we allow ourselves the space and time to contemplate what permeated the sabbath rest taken by those women: the impending somber trek to a tomb still filled, the final anointing of a beloved teacher who now lay stone-cold?

Such rest prevents our taking tomorrow for granted in our lives and in our churches. Such rest helps us recognize that we discern the sacramental possibility of Holy Saturday in quiet contemplation of God's presence even in the face of death.

On Saturday, the women rest. In their resting we find the seeds that prepare them to be first witnesses of the unexpected joy that the day following sabbath brings.

Find a time and space apart this day to rest. Reflect on what weighed on those women in their rest. How can their sabbath vigil deepen our faith?

Fleeting Recognition
(Easter Sunday)

Read Luke 24:13-33.

Loaf and cup are blessed. Seated in the pew, processing to the chancel, or kneeling at the rail, you hear words offered that call to mind something other than morsels of bread and tastes of wine or juice. *Let this be to you according to your faith the body and blood of Christ.* In the best of such moments, you recognize the mystery of Christ's presence. And "he is risen!" flows as naturally as breathing.

But even the most mystical experience of this meal does not linger for long. Cloth covers chalice and paten, a reminder of what the tomb's first visitors saw where the body should have been. A song is sung, as a song once marked the interval between upper room and Gethsemane. And then? Then you walk outside, into a world that largely presumes bread is just bread and juice is just juice—and where *Christ is risen* seems untenable in light of daily testaments that death has not yielded many resurrections of late.

You might sense that faith engendered in cross-illuminated worship seems fleeting. You would be right. But that is nothing new. Luke embeds this sense of "fleetingness" throughout his account of the Emmaus story. Bear in mind that the root word for fleeting implies movement: *flee.* As the story begins, two disciples flee Jerusalem. They move away from this week's confusion. An unrecognized stranger joins them and sheds light on the events that have left them bewildered. Only at table, in the blessing, breaking, and giving of the bread does recognition finally dawn. And then, just as quickly, the One who effected that recognition vanishes—a *fleeting* discernment of holy presence. And what results from it? Once again, these two *flee*. But now they flee not *from* Jerusalem but *toward* community.

So it goes in worship practiced in light of the cross. So it goes in every sacramental encounter of the crucified and risen Jesus. Moments of sacred discernment and mystical clarity come in just that way: moments. The recognition of holy presence in morsels of bread and sips of wine or juice are fleeting because they set us back on the road nourished with the news and hope of resurrection, however hidden that news or distant that hope may seem at this juncture. Worship is not our permanent domicile; it is our departure gate.

This book's journey through worship transformed in light of the cross draws to a fitting close on Easter. It is fitting because without a cross there would be no need for raising. But your journey of living transformed in light of the cross is only beginning. May those Emmaus disciples guide your steps. Their recognition of a soon-to-vanish Jesus testifies that cross-formed faith, like cross-formed worship, does not set anchor in ecstatic vision but propels disciples into community and world. Why? There is news to tell and service to render: *Christ is risen!*

Holy God, open me to your presence in sacrament, in neighbor, in stranger. Amen.

LEADER'S GUIDE

The following two pages provide an outline that you may copy for use in planning each of the six suggested sessions. The pages after the outline contain specific ideas for each week: suggestions for engaging participants in that week's materials and theme. Feel free to adapt the suggested session ideas to meet the needs and interests of your group. Blend and incorporate the activities and exercises suggested with your own ideas for how best to lead each session in your particular setting.

You will notice a strong emphasis on worship by having each session open and close with an act of worship and by creating a weekly Worship Center that offers a focal point for that week's engagements with the theme and readings. That emphasis is intentional in order to ground these sessions in devotional *practices* more than simply *conversations* about worship. I strongly encourage you to incorporate a cross or crucifix into each Worship Center.

Distribute the books a minimum of one week ahead of the first session, with clear instructions to read the Foreword and do the first week's daily readings (one per day) **prior** to the first session. As this group experience is set within Lent, you might even consider holding a brief meeting on Ash Wednesday (perhaps after your church's observance of its ritual) where you distribute the books and provide the instructions indicated above. If you do that, you may choose to read together the Ash Wednesday reading and use the prayer at its end for a commissioning of this group experience.

SESSION OUTLINE

Preparation

(Gathering and arranging what you will need for this session)

- Create a Worship Center (*expressive of week's theme*).
- Gather materials needed for Worship Center and session activities.

Gathering

(Creating a worshipful and welcoming setting for participants)

- Welcome participants, and lead a community-building activity.
- Begin with an opening ritual that connects Worship Center elements with week's theme.

Reflecting

(Exploring this week's element of worship)

- Invite and discuss participants' reactions to and questions evoked by the readings.
- Use discussion questions/activities leader brings.

Responding

(Incorporating insights into individual and congregational life)

- Identify ways to engage this element of worship in personal discipleship.
- Consider possibilities for renewing congregational life through this element of worship.

Commissioning

(Encouraging fresh practice of this element of cross-formed worship)

- Note any closing thoughts and/or commitments to action.
- Use the Liturgy of Sending to help move participants from session to discipleship.

IDEAS FOR WEEK ONE

Worship Center Ideas (including a cross)

- Symbols that signify welcome, particularly in your community and church and candle in this and following sessions to symbolize light of cross
- Images or pictures of various community gatherings

Gathering Options

- Participants identify personal experiences that served to gather them in community.
- Light candle and say aloud this invocation, "We are all one in Christ Jesus." Have a second person join you in saying that, then a third, and so on until everyone's voice in the group has been added.

Discussion Questions and Activities

- Lead a discussion based on the exercise at the close of "If and Then" (page 18).
- Journal thoughts on what boundaries are most detrimental in your church and community.
- Share an experience where a faith community has helped transform your life.

Congregational Connection Possibilities

- Talk about how your church's liturgy and physical environment helps form community.
- Identify ways your church can more proactively invite and welcome folks.

Considerations for Commissioning

- Encourage participants to begin each day this week by reflecting on what being gathered into a community that worships in light of the cross can make on their lives that day.

- Lead a litany whose unison refrain is the prayer that closes "Transformed Relationship."

IDEAS FOR WEEK TWO

Worship Center Ideas (including a cross)

- Candle and lighter
- Index cards or pictures that contain or depict different names or metaphors for God

Gathering Options

- Light candle to signify God's presence, and share experiences of standing on holy ground.
- Choose a card or picture from the Worship Center. Lead a round-robin invocation: Each says aloud, "We gather in the name of . . ." and finishes with name/metaphor they have chosen.

Discussion Questions and Activities

- Have individuals choose one of the three concluding questions in "Who Is This?" (page 34).
- Form three groups, one for each of the questions chosen above, and discuss ways to incorporate that question in a personal spiritual discipline this week.

Congregational Connection Possibilities

- Discuss how your congregation bids attention to Holy Presence in worship and service.
- Use the reflective question that closes "The Anointed" (page 38) to identify ways your church can equip folks to be mindful of the cross-formed implications of invoking Christ.

Considerations for Commissioning

- Have participants identify one thing they will carry with them from this session.

- Repeat three times in unison the prayer that concludes "Who Is This?" (page 34): the first time, at a normal volume; the second time, more softly; the third time, in a whisper.

IDEAS FOR WEEK THREE

Worship Center Ideas (including a cross)

- Blank sheets of paper and markers and/or other art supplies
- Candle and lighter

Gathering Options

- Using paper and art supplies, ask each participant to create an image of what he or she would most want to bring to God's attention this day (no words, please).

- Light the candle, then ask participants to place images one at a time on the Worship Center. As each is placed, lead the group in the following response: *Receive this prayer, O God, and the one who brings it to you.*

Discussion Questions and Activities

- Discuss how shame, pride, and fear get in the way of participants' honesty to God.

- Journal thoughts and commitment to act based on the closing exercise in "Intercession" (page 50).

Congregational Connection Possibilities

- Review the second paragraph of the overview (page 43), and discuss how your congregation can broaden the practice of confession in worship.

- Identify ways your congregation supports those whose life experiences leave them wondering, *Is anybody there?*

Considerations for Commissioning

- Invite participants to reflect one of their spiritual practices that would benefit from greater honesty to God. Challenge them to work on that in the coming week.

- Close with sentence prayers offered by individuals.

IDEAS FOR WEEK FOUR

Worship Center Ideas (including a cross)

- Banner to display on worship center, containing quote often attributed to Saint Francis: "Preach the gospel at all times, if necessary, use words."
- Markers; newsprint sheet headlined at top: "This church proclaims the gospel by. . . ."
- Candle and lighter

Gathering Options

- Ask participants to write on the newsprint their completions of that sentence.
- Light the candle and offer a prayer that seeks the leading of God's Spirit in this session.

Discussion Questions and Activities

- Use the opening paragraph in "Discerning the Season" (page 61) to guide a conversation on the importance of discerning timeliness when it comes to proclaiming and living the gospel.
- Suggest that partners share thoughts generated by the closing questions for "Bottom Lines" (page 68).

Congregational Connection Possibilities

- Reflecting on the overview (page 57), identify ways your congregation currently encourages and equips laity to proclaim the gospel—and new ways it can do so.

- Use the concluding reflection question in "Afflicting the Comfortable" (page 66) to explore what might be hard—but needed—for your church to hear and/or speak in the current moment.

Considerations for Commissioning

- Invite participants to identify one affirmation or question this session raises for them.
- Form a circle. Turn to the person on your right, and say, *(Name), Christ calls you to proclaim the gospel.* That person then turns to the right and repeats these words to the next in line. The process continues until all participants have been commissioned.

IDEAS FOR WEEK FIVE

Worship Center Ideas (including a cross)

- Copies of various creeds and statements of faith (your hymnal may be a good source)
- Paper and pens for journal exercise
- Copies of church budget
- Candle and lighter

Gathering Options

- Ask participants to review individually the closing exercise in "An Astonishing Thing" (page 78) and to identify one bedrock principle of faith.
- Light the candle and lead a prayer of invocation by beginning with "We gather in this faith, O God" followed by participants' naming the principle most central to their faith.

Discussion Questions and Activities

- Reflect on and journal responses to the closing prayer of "Follow-Through" (page 74).
- In small groups, discuss the closing questions of "We Shall Not Fear" (page 80).

Congregational Connection Possibilities

- If you do the small-group discussion of "We Shall Not Fear," lead the group in a conversation on how the church can help individuals to own "we shall not fear."
- Distribute copies of your church's budget. Discuss how expenditures reflect the faith your congregation "owns."

Considerations for Commissioning

- Have participants recall their principle of faith named in the invocation. Invite brief responses on anything in this session that will help them own that principle in daily life.

- Unite in praying the Lord's Prayer, and encourage folks to own the faith this prayer confesses.

IDEAS FOR WEEK SIX

Worship Center Ideas (including a cross)

- Symbols or artwork that are suggestive of something that cannot be fully seen, such as a door that is only partly open, leaving viewer to wonder what lies beyond it; path leading over a hill and/or winding out of sight
- Construction paper, scissors, pencils
- Candle and lighter

Gathering Options

- Have participants trace around the edges of their feet on paper and cut out a pair of footprints. Ask them to write on one side of each footprint a decision they face about the future.
- Light the candle and offer an opening prayer that seeks God's leading in this time together.

Discussion Questions and Activities

- Discuss the reflective questions at the end of "Fieldwork" (page 94). Individually or in small groups, reinforce participants' commitment to carrying out one act this week.
- Have participants write on the other side of their footprints how faith encourages them to step out in hope in that decision.

Congregational Connection Possibilities

- Consider the reflection questions at the end of "Disturbers of the Peace" (page 96). Identify the ways your church does or might encourage or join with those who engage in such action on behalf of others.

Considerations for Commissioning

- Invite participants to lift up what they have found most valuable in this session, and overall in these gatherings. Thank them for their participation.

- Suggest that individuals come forward, one at a time, to place their footprints on or around the Worship Center. The group repeats this unison blessing for each individual: *(Name), in God's hands, enter the future with hope.*

NOTES

1. Fyodor Dostoevsky, *The Brothers Karamazov*, trans. Richard Pevear (NY: Farrar, Straus and Giroux, 2002), 583.

2. Bryan Stevenson, *Just Mercy: A Story of Justice and Redemption* (NY: Spiegel & Grau, 2015).

3. Elie Wiesel, *Night*, trans. Marion Wiesel (NY: Hill and Wang, 2006), 65.

About the Author

════════════

John Indermark is a writer and retired United Church of Christ minister. He is the author of a number of books published by Upper Room Books and Abingdon Press and has also written for a variety of curriculum resources. John and his wife, Judy, split their time between the Sonoran desert region of Tucson and the Willapa Hills rainforest in southwest Washington.

CPSIA information can be obtained
at www.ICGtesting.com
Printed in the USA
FSOW04n1659270117
30070FS